CONVIVIAL

A Quest for the Masterpiece Within

VOLUME I

Cheryl Chavarria

Visit & Subscribe
www.theconvivialwoman.com

Contact
If you have any questions or comments,
email info@theconvivialwoman.com

Facebook
www.facebook.com/theconvivialwoman

Twitter
@cherylchavarria

Table of Contents

"The dreams of my heart are the dreams of the universe dreaming through me."

—Julia Cameron

Introduction

I'm Cheryl Chavarria, writer and creator of The Convivial Woman, an online haven for conscious creators and convivial living.

If your goal is to experience personal fulfillment, whether creatively, spiritually, or emotionally, and work to uncover and master your talents to create change in the world, then you are in the right place.

For the past couple of years, I have devoted my writing (read: life) to understanding and experiencing this peculiar and undeniable connection between creativity, spirituality, and our shared humanity.

We now live in a world that requires us to rise up from the mundane routines and preconditioned thinking and to take a more proactive approach to living our lives as conscious, convivial creators.

When you think about the words "art", "creative," or "creator,"—what comes to mind? Is it someone standing at an easel, ready to paint as Picasso and Dali once did? Someone sitting at a kitchen table writing the first draft of a great story as Stephen King continually does? Or do you envision the Mona Lisa or any of the other world masterpieces lining the walls of Le Louvre in Paris?

Those impressions are pretty common and tend to make people feel isolated and discouraged from pursuing anything creative, or even thinking to have the *audacity* to call themselves as such, because they find it hard to view themselves on the same level, in the same light.

Art is less about the canvas you have mounted on your wall, though, or the classics lining your bookshelves, and more about the ways in which you deliver your interpretation of the world around you. It's what I consider to be *the art of convivial living*.

It's a way of life, the moments of bliss you make time to see, feel, hear, taste, smell, and touch. It's when you make the everyday choice, whether subtle or profound, to live your life with passion and according to your own design. It's the pleasure and freedom to create for a living, or simply as a means to express yourself. It's operating at your soul's level and behaving as children do… absorbing, experimenting, fumbling, questioning, interacting, trusting, imagining, loving, and playing in this world with each opportunity you're given to do so.

This state of being is a matter of expressing your instinct to play, to trust in and be led by curiosity. It's the belief that in order to truly live and feel alive...you must create. Art in all its forms—writing, painting, negotiating, drawing, jewelry-making, photographing, acting, or brand-new business hatching—is the vehicle, the mode of transportation that your soul uses to make the journey from the depths of who you are to the outside world. Simply put…

Art is when you hear a knocking from your soul—and you answer.

—Terri Guillemets

I implore you to open that imaginary door to yourself.

All the love in my heart,

Cheryl

Prelude to
the Convivial
Revolution

How Are You Living?

Right now, you could be living in one world. Yet, the moment you decide you're done with it, ready for a change, then with fierce determination, your mind fires up to design a new experience.

One example of that is your choice to acquire this book and consider entering into the *Convivial Collective*—a community of people who hold a deep desire to explore, discover, and act on their one call to action in this lifetime. It's the call to create a *convivial life*, one that involves walking your own path, discovering your own truths, following your heart's desires, exercising your unique creative abilities, mastering your true strengths, and serving the world as a result of it all. What you do after putting this book down is what determines your commitment to the quality of your life's unique design.

By showing up to this page, these words, and this idea of living more in integrity with your personal beliefs and desires, you officially place your name on a roster of creative, courageous kinfolk. You are ready for meaningful change.

Perhaps the time has come for you to put yourself first so you can truly offer your best to others. Is it time to shed those self-conscious tendencies coming from a not-so-enlightened upbringing? How about that search for love in all the wrong places…are you prepared to turn up the volume on personal responsibility to your own happiness and let love notice you?

Meaningful change is forgetting the talk and putting on your fuck it shoes to finally walk the walk.

It could be ending your days as a self-sacrificing do-gooder and experiencing fulfillment when you say "No, thank you." We could be talking about a complete do-over as it relates to your response to life and the ways in which you engage in it.

When you make the move to acknowledge your heart's incessant yearnings and demonstrate the will to pursue them, you soon find yourself consumed by the courage and freedom to LIVE them.

We are fed all of these messages growing up that do nothing to encourage us to venture out and take an exploratory approach to living. I'm here to let you know that the world is here for you, waiting for you to immerse yourself in it...to see, taste, feel, breathe, admire, walk, climb, drive, fly over, lay on, dig your feet into, curl your toes under, and adorn yourself with it. Why aren't you doing it, more often, as often as you can?

What Do You Aspire For?

For material possessions? For titles and certifications? While they are fulfilling endeavors, it's easy to lose sight of why you may be pursuing more education and experience. It's not to set yourself apart from others, but to grant yourself the expertise and ability to serve and share your experience with others.

What you want to create—whether it is a new life, career, book, a baby, a business, or even a place to call home—is worth the fight. Many times, there will be a fight because such transformative decisions naturally go against the norm. Many times, the battle is within you. Be strong and know that you are meant for greatness, to create a lasting impact and to leave a legacy.

I want to thank you for saying yes to this convivial experience; it's the beginning of many as you set out on this new journey. To welcome you and help light the way, I've spent much time pouring my heart into the material that awaits you on the pages ahead. It's all with the desire to contribute what I can to what's already brewing deep within you.

This book is my creation, my gift to you, and its message now ventures into your hands with the desire to enlighten, restore, and transform you in whatever way you see fit.

See the world from a convivial perspective starting *now*.

In a 2001 interview with Barbara Walters, I heard Julia Roberts first utter the word "Convivial" to describe her experience working with the cast of *Ocean's Eleven*. I'd never known of a word that sounded like this before and hearing how it could be used to sum up an entire experience proved to be a lasting memory. That one word was destined to open up a whole new world for me.

As writer and creator of The Convivial Woman, I have come to believe that this word perfectly describes the state of mind and lifestyle every person seeks. It best represents your spirit, talents, and intentions here on earth. It's a guiding light that can lead you down a path *all your own*…if you are willing to spark the fire within you.

One Word For It All

This book is my initial declaration on what the word convivial means to me and what it can potentially mean for you.

I have weaved together stories from my own experience along with down-to-earth guidance, insights and exercises to inspire you to begin your quest to awaken the *living* work of art in you.

You are here because your dreams are *your* priority and you know that your life is *your* responsibility. There is a voice inside calling you home to who you truly are. Perhaps you're starting to hear it more and more and by taking steps to convert the faint echoes in your heart to a lifestyle all your own—a convivial one—you are fulfilling an innate desire within you that constantly craves your energy and attention.

It is your right to heed the direction of your heart, even if in many instances it doesn't make sense to you, to others, or doesn't feel comfortable. There is no one goal we aspire to except to develop and express the one thing *you* were born to do. It's that one thing you are driven to do, that keeps you up at night, that brings you and others joy, that gives back to the world around you because it expresses the very essence of who you are.

What can the word CONVIVIAL **mean for your life? How can it begin to represent** YOUR **spirit? How can** YOU **use it as a guide, as a chosen way to approach and view your life?**

This journey began for me because of my desire to write and to accomplish the feat of every conscious, creative person…self-actualization. I share my transition from people-pleaser and permission-seeker to convivial woman and defiant creator. I talk about how I rose above conventional wisdom because it didn't fully nurture and support my spirit. I decided to create a new story for myself, one that continually evolves, and one to which I'm fully committed. You can do the same.

The pages ahead have one underlying theme in each story I share—CHOICE. When it comes to the design and experience of your life, the choice belongs to you. What you want matters and I want to empower you to let your desires ride shotgun as you sit behind the wheel of your life and drive with conviction.

An important aspect to convivial living is taking the time to cultivate a close connection with your inner muse, with what inspires you to create. The muse is your constant companion on this journey back to you and it will serve you well as you endeavor to courageously share the true version of who you are with the world.

Walking a new path is bound to bring you feelings of discomfort coupled with exhilaration, because this is the experience of living from pure will, instinct, and desire. It can be a challenging, confusing, and emotionally charged existence, but I guarantee you a transformational and powerful experience. And isn't that how you want to experience life, anyway? Dearest work of art…it's time to begin living accordingly.

There is a desired and deserving life experience for every human being. It is a life inspired by all that gives you the freedom to be at home with yourself and others. It's what I deem as…

The Art of Convivial Living

This is the overall idea that I discuss in my blog and there is no one way to define it, because it is unique—unique to you.

When I think of the art of convivial living, I envision a person putting a close ear to the faint whispers of their heart, reaching deep within the recesses of their imagination to bring forth into reality a life experience only they can create.

When operating on this level, you are someone who acts with conviction, who plays in the world as you did as a child—without fear, without inhibition; without worry about what people thought of you, without hesitation to just be you. There is no thinking in this realm of living, only feeling. That's not to say that you don't use your mind to make decisions. No…it means you base your decisions on how you feel, and if the feeling is good—and there's no contracting or holding back—then you act, you move forward. Don't confuse this for any narcissistic endeavor, though. The purpose must include serving others. In considering one another, the world's a more convivial place because of our collective aspirations and efforts.

As a result of my own intention to practice the art of convivial living, this book began with the sole purpose to encourage you to uncover and create the solutions, experiences, relationships, and opportunities that can make your spirit rise to the surface, allowing you to have the impact only you can have on this world

Being the star of any show is not a role for which I ever auditioned…until now. I've asked myself plenty of times, "How do you take something so

Breaking Ground

private, like your writing, your art, something so intimate, spiritual and close to you, and make it public?"

As a writer, a creator of any kind, it's a daunting task that feels very exposing, but when you are compelled, called to action, you just do it because you know you have to share it so the world can benefit from it. The same thing goes for what wants to be created in you.

The light is bound to shine on you, but it takes courage and desire to take the stage. The audience awaits your unique performance. It's simply a matter of when you're willing to step forward.

A Time For Everything

Being the observer, a consumer of the world around you has its purpose: for enjoying and taking in the moment, for gathering material for your next project. Then, a switch must occur and there comes a time to act, perform, even direct, so you may contribute what is unique to you and be of service to another.

It is at that moment that you must push past your fears of rejection, lack of love, and judgment in order to step out from behind the curtain to take your occasional bow, cause some laughter, shed some tears, take in applause, glimpse a few yawns, hear potential boos and face numerous critics. This is the drama of life in its many forms and we must participate in it and play our parts well, and even be willing to don new costumes and personas if need be. It's our need to adapt and continually reinvent ourselves.

Deciding on your life's direction forces you to stand firm in who you are because if you want to **make any desire a reality**, you have to accept the natural fear, raw emotions, and the sense of vulnerability you experience with any new path you venture down. You lose nothing and gain all the experience. Your life and the lives of those affected are richer as a result of your courageous choices and the effort you put into them.

Take Your Proper Place In Life

So, how do you begin to take the wheel and change direction or set out on an entirely new path?

First, acknowledge what you want to change. Then consider the reasons why you want or need this change. You could seek out a close confidant to peel back the layers of the situation to get a good understanding of it and how to move beyond it, but do your best to not start any unhealthy patterns of repetitive venting and complaining. It feels good at first to let it out with someone, but that could get old and bring about little progress.

The action always falls back on you, so why not share your innermost feelings with a blank page or try to sort it out between you and the muse through a more creative outlet?

Do you seize random opportunities to connect with yourself? Do you soak in hot steamy baths (Himalayan bath salts smelling of lavender, anyone?), or how about long walks by yourself? Do you take advantage of empty red swings under weeping willow trees?

Whatever form you seek to connect with yourself and commune with the world around you, indulge in that activity, steal those moments for yourself.

It's in those moments when you recall memories, sentiments that rekindle joy or help you discover new ways to engage in your life. You never know when or how epiphanies will hit, so put yourself in position to receive, hear, or be blindsided by them. Yes, sometimes they can come that forcefully.

Take the time for you. That's it. And do what you want. Or do nothing at all. Sometimes that's what you need. Stop running on the hamster wheel, striving so hard to figure things out and just get out and live.

It's is in these ordinary moments of time alone, of engagement, of play, of solitude that a kind of clearing takes place: the path spanning before you mysteriously gets dusted off and you're soon able to see where to take your next step.

You open up some doorway in your mind for solutions to walk through about how to plan your exit, afford the house, dump the loser, forgive yourself, start the business, make the cash flow, set the date, make the move, shed the baggage, resolve the conflict.

Sometimes it means surrendering the fight and accepting what needs to end in order for a new beginning to materialize. If you never let go, you won't know what it's like to come off the ground and get a bird's-eye view of the new world that awaits you.

You can peruse the pages of myriad self-help books, denounce the negative and only choose to see the positive, subscribe to the philosophies of spiritual teachers and random gurus alike, but if you're consuming it all and not bothering to make any real strokes to the canvas of your real life, then what's the use?

The answers already exist within you, so don't hesitate to believe your own voice and listen to it.

Great Power Is the Reality of Our Existence

Isn't it funny how intimidating and scary it can feel to simply acknowledge that we are powerful and can be wildly successful if we want? Such fears are a normal part of the process of aspiring to realize one's potential. There's always going to be doubt lurking in the background, trying to convince you that you don't know what you're doing, you don't know who you are or what you want.

There will be plenty of sentiments like that when you set your sights on a less conventional path, but this is where outrageous self-belief, your personal experience, and your closest confidants who get you enter the scene. They are there to help you combat self-sabotage and push forward with the ambitions of your heart. Instead of trying to become, you aspire to simply be. By trusting in yourself, you get to know this power of yours—what it feels like, looks like, and sounds like. The people you attract into your social hemisphere are there to offer you what you need, especially when you aren't aware of what or how much of it you need. They should offer you the space and freedom to open up so that your tender skin can be fully revealed.

Be willing to ask questions and have conversations that cause you to sweat out your insecurities and render you completely vulnerable. The power is in your hands to curate your life, to make choices that reassure you that you're exactly where you need to be, doing what you want to do, living how you intend to live.

Is Life For You Or Against You? The Choice Is Yours

Instead of feeling like life is happening to you, find ways to think and behave more proactively so you can make life happen for you. To start, you'll need to begin evaluating your life in its current state.

What do you like about it?

Can you see yourself in it?

Where do you see need for change?

How honest are you with others, with yourself?

By keeping your eyes fixed on the needlepoint of your inner compass, you can make all the difference in your life's direction.

In larger things, we are convivial;
what causes trouble is the trivial.

—Richard Armour

On The
Word
Convivial

The foundation of anything is its belief system, or as author Simon Sinek has recently popularized, your why. So what is the belief system that goes into living a convivial life? First, let's define the word Convivial. Back at Merriam-Webster's, I am told the following:

YOU

Convivial

[kuhn-viv-ee-uhl]:

Fond of feasting, drinking, and good company; jovial; of or befitting a feast; festive; folksy, forthcoming, affable, genial, kindly, lively, communicative, expansive, high-spirited.

Most people understand this word as a way to paint a merry, jovial, happy, atmosphere, an over-all good time, and isn't that what you seek in your every day life—to commune with others as the person you are naturally? When things get hectic, stressful, mundane or routine, you seek an outlet. That outlet is the route you take to reach *your* version and vision for that jovial state of mind and living. To be more specific,

CONVIVIAL is who you are, at the core, deep inside.

You are convivial. Yes, you. It's a more precise way to describe your spirit engaged, *in action*. Of course, there is *no one way* to express yourself. Everyone's idea, interpretation and demonstration of that word in their lives will be different in appearance but similar in intention.

I believe we are all seeds originating from a Great Creator and seeds are not meant to be idle. They are meant to dwell in fertile soil, to be nourished, given light, so they can shift, grow, expand, transform, and experience change from one form to another, and another, until they reach their full potential. Look to nature for your example of how to live your life.

You are someone who wants to recognize and remember why you're here.

The answer:

to create, experience, and experiment; to serve and share the abundant talents and generous spirit that makes up who you are.
All without guilt.

You have unique strengths and there are unlimited realms in which your mind wishes to engage. You believe in trusting and letting intuition guide you. It's an aspect of your-self, of a subconscious, mysterious, and in many instances, unknown and undiscovered part of your existence. It is a source waiting for you to connect to it because it has the same intention…to help you express the living work of art that makes you you.

You've seen enough people, even if distant examples in books, on TV, films, or real life, and you see how they've made it possible to create a life around their talents. Perhaps you feel your time is coming, or maybe it's already here. Your thoughts should be geared toward the idea, *If they can do it, why not me?*

Who is a Creator?

Artists come in all forms: however, calling yourself such, dressing the part, or learning the lingo is not what makes one an artist. The work they do is what grants them that state of being.

Being an artist *is a way* of thinking and living.

These are folks who exercise a convivial mindset in every aspect of their life. Their goal is to lead a fun-filled, passionate, and rich existence. If convivial means that you're fond of feasting, drinking, and good company, or expressing your jovial nature, then what is the one thing in life that you can aspire to *do* in order to *embody* and present as an *offering* to the world so your convivial nature can be put on display?

What do you need to reach such a mindset? You need to do what you love, pursue what your heart yearns for, and you must live it. Every day.

WORKSHEET

Manifesting Qualities of a Convivial Creator

They are:
1. Curious
2. Creative
3. Proactive

They have:
1. Outrageous Self-Belief
2. Unrelenting Optimism

See yourself above? If so, how? Write down some examples of how you already manifest these qualities in your life.

_____

_____

_____

_____

_____

_____

_____

_____

_____

_____

_____

_____

WORKSHEET

If not, write out how you can begin to incorporate these qualities more often. Pick a problem, some obstacle, a concern, or situation you feel *may* be out of your control, and think about ways you can approach it with the above characteristics and see what results may come of it.

Example: Are you a parent with a teenage son who isn't listening to you, wants to do his own thing? If you're not getting through to him, who do you know who can possibly offer their influence and advice? What materials can you seek to help you? It takes a village, remember.

Or, what if you're at a job you don't want to be at any longer? You've given them all you have, your loyalty, flexibility, expertise, but they just aren't showing that they value you or your work. What steps can you take to create momentum toward a new work environment?

Brainstorm your personal scenarios below.

SCENARIO 1:

_____

_____

_____

_____

_____

_____

_____

_____

SCENARIO 2:

_____

_____

_____

_____

_____

_____

_____

_____

SCENARIO 3:

_____

_____

_____

_____

_____

_____

_____

_____

Redefining
Art,One
Convivial Act
At A Time

Creativity is not what most people think it may be. It's an enlightened version of problem solving, a game of connecting the dots while blindfolded. It is your interpretation of life as you are living it. It's seeking personal evolution in order to contribute to the world.

It's not just about art. It's about freedom, the freedom to be you, to express you. That's what life is truly about, that's what humans constantly crave—freedom to be, to do. How do you feel when you're being and expressing you? Convivial! Art is simply the vehicle, the mode of transportation that your soul takes from the depths of who you are to the outside world.

Think of every well-known artist who intrigues you. Are you on that roster of Greats? Many times, it's hard to visualize or even feel comfortable with calling ourselves artists, but that's because most of us think to use that word to describe something relating to the visual arts. There is so much more to it.

Here's the truth: I'm no different than the Greats and neither are you.

A work of art resides within us all. It's simply a matter of time, awareness and effort before an awakening can occur to express the creative genius in you.

Once you see yourself as an artist, a creator in your own right, only then can you pursue the visions and worlds forming within you and attract who and what you need to create a life around it.

To bust through any form of creative self-limitation, you must first consider and question the definitions of art.

Wikipedia says

Art is the product or process of deliberately arranging items (often with symbolic significance) in a way that influences and affects one or more of the senses, emotions, and intellect...

Britannica Online defines art as

the use of skill and imagination in the creation of aesthetic objects, environments, or experiences that can be shared with others.

Goethe defined art as...

a second nature.

I want you to consider a more expanded version of what the "A"-word means because it encompasses aspects of living that are so fundamental to growth and happiness.

THE CONVIVIAL WOMAN'S DEFINITION OF
ART IS ANYTHING YOU…

love,
imagine,
desire,
play,
design,
interpret,
express,
reveal,
practice,
teach.

ART IS THE **<u>ACT</u>** OF DISCOVERING **<u>YOURSELF</u>**…

Art…act…yourself.

Where does art play its many roles in your life? Think you've been
practicing the art of convivial living all this time without realizing it?
I'm sure you've got some creative victories under your belt by now.

How Do You Engage In Art?

Referring back to Goethe and The Convivial Woman's definition of art, take this time to consider how you may be artistically engaging in your life. Give specific examples of each action that comes to you naturally.

Love _____

Imagine _____

Desire _____

Play _____

Design _____

Interpret _____

Express _____

Reveal _____

Practice _____

Teach _____

When you begin to see art in the list above, you come to see how many avenues of self-expression you have to choose from. The playing field between you and the masters has just been leveled.

Still see yourself any less capable than the artists that came before you? They had the same number of hours in the day to work as you do and the same brain structure and anatomy as you. Perhaps, the resources differed but remember, only the resourceful thrive. You are just as capable of mastering your talents and serving up some beauty for this world to feast its eyes on.

The business of creating, of painting yourself as a natural-born artist, is the business of sharing your interpretation and experience of Life. If you enjoy experiencing the mind, talent, and voice of another, why not offer up your own take?

How The Creative Process Feels

This convivial guide has been long in the making, but guess why it had not come to pass? Fear. Intimidation. Uncertainty. Worrying too much about the how instead of focusing on the why.

I allowed fear and uncertainty to plague my efforts and wasn't sure when I'd get serious about organizing my thoughts into an actual book, so I let time slip away, but never the desire to do it. However, I must note:

Desire alone produces nothing.

When you're walking your own path, such emotions are constant companions, but the more practice you get with taking risks and facing your fears, the more you learn to move past them.

In the beginning stages of creation, it can feel like you're fumbling your way through a pitch-black room, looking for the light switch, but the faith you have in finding your way through it all is the one factor that helps you to arrive at creative fruition.

When it comes to creating anything in your life, one crucial thing to remember is...it could be great, it could be shit. But regardless, it's up to you whether *it* will exist.

We tend to beat ourselves up for not getting what we want done, but there is a divine timing to things that you must trust. If you stay in the game—and you must!—everything will come together.

Turning Pain Into Power

Your experiences can be transferred from one form to another by engaging in creative acts. Pain and adversity can become something from which others can learn.

When you're willing to let your guard down, declare what you need, admit that you don't know what to do or where to turn, this is the point where you can bear witness to the intersection of beauty, humility and grace within. You can take this experience further by taking the initiative to capture it if you choose to on paper, canvas, or by creating a unique experience for others to engage in.

Many of us walk around trying to hold ourselves together when the foundation of our lives is on the brink of collapse. We don't want to let anyone in for fear of being seen as dramatic, needy, emotional, and vulnerable. But isn't that how we are literally born into this world? Throughout life, we learn to put up walls and fronts and plaster on smiles to portray the picture perfect life, but living on the surface is far from a festive experience.

You may feel like a fraud, phony, half-hearted, like you need to run for cover so you can finally stop holding your breath. This is not the way, this is not convivial living. Honesty and integrity to oneself and expressing your vulnerable nature through art and living life is where the treasures await you.

Self-doubt can be an ally...it serves as an indicator of aspiration. It reflects love of something we dream of doing, and desire to do it. If you find yourself asking yourself (and your friends), 'Am I really a writer? Am I really an artist?' chances are you are.

—Steven Pressfield, The War of Art

Doubt Can Be Useful

What do you doubt, question, or find yourself on the fence about when it comes to the messages and methods you've been taught on how to design your life, around your creative gifts, concerning your dreams?

Welcome your doubts versus shying away from them and thinking that certainty is the best way to go. If we didn't doubt, there would be no reason to question, and if we don't question, how can we grow as individuals and how could change find its way into our lives and the world? Doubt shapes you and molds your life into something uniquely yours.

Self-inquiry is crucial if you want to live a fulfilling life. You have to keep yourself at the forefront of every decision you make, but without knowing yourself well enough and all that moves you, as well as everything that doesn't, you can't ensure your decisions will always lead you where you want them to.

Your Convivial Nature

Let's get to know a few words we often hear just a little better. We may think we know what "nature" and "essence" mean, but sometimes that can be taken for granted if we don't take the time to truly dig deep and find out what they can mean for our lives and how we design them. According to Merriam-Webster online…

Nature [na cher]:

an inherent character or basic constitution of a person or thing; a creative and controlling force in the universe. An inner force or the sum of such forces in an individual. A kind or class usually distinguished by fundamental characteristics; the physical constitution or drives of an organism; a spontaneous attitude; the external world in its entirety; humankind's original or natural condition; a simplified mode of life.

Synonyms: genius, character, self.

Essence \'e-sə n(t)s\

The most significant quality, element, or aspect of a thing; in or by its very nature. Related words: heart, spirit, center, core, embodiment, epitome, incarnation, manifestation, personification, aspect, attribute.

No Coincidences

I can't help noticing the flow, the order, and sequence of visuals I get when pondering the word *nature*. I look it up in the dictionary only to find a related word—*evoke*. I look up that word's meaning, only to be led to *vocation*, only to be led to *voice*. This isn't a coincidence that all of these words bring about the same feeling, perhaps even the same result when you allow them to guide you.

It is in your *nature* to be convivial; when you listen to the call of your heart, the *voice* within leads you to your *vocation*, your unique calling and it evokes the work of art in you.

All of the words above share the root – they are grammatical forms of the same word, the Latin *"Voce"* – voice/calling. The affixation changes depending on what we do with that "voice."

Words We Take For Granted

At the start of 2009, I attended a taping for a local Dallas woman's TV show and the guest she interviewed was the author of a relationship book written to enlighten women on how to understand the ways in which men express love. Feeling generous, the author decided to play Oprah and gave copies away to every person in the audience. The ladies in attendance were ecstatic. He did it wholeheartedly because he said that he believed sharing the book was part of his *personal ministry.*

*Ministry…*the word struck me funny and gave me a new feeling compared to my strict Christian upbringing. I wondered, *So what does the word Ministry entail, anyway?* Many times, we understand what a word means, but looking up its actual origin and meaning can bring new life to our understanding of it. So I looked it up at Merriam-Webster where I always go.

Ministry: a person or thing through which something is accomplished.

Minister: a person sent on a mission to represent another.

Minister to: to attend to the needs and comforts of…

It was always hard for me to pin down a quick answer when someone would ask me, "What do you write?" or "What is this website of yours about?"

I was hesitant to be boxed into one category of topics, because my journey to dig deep within and better know the person I am happened through the words that flowed out of me. What I wrote landed onto the page untamed and not necessarily finished.

There is something mystical about revealing yourself, baring it all in front of people. You show up, let your guard down and wait to be moved, heard, understood, and seen. This is what the call to create and the pursuit of a convivial life does for you if you're up for the challenge. It humbles you and gives you the opportunity to practice a form of devotion and commitment to nurturing yourself. It ignites the creator in you and compels you to then give it away in myriad forms.

Getting a more in-depth understanding of the word ministry allowed me to see my efforts as the creator of The Convivial Woman as a form of my own personal ministry.

WORKSHEET

What's Your Ministry? Life Purpose?

What ministry is yours to claim? How can you begin to uncover your life's purpose? Here's a starting point to consider where your passions may intersect:

What expertise do you have already?

_____

_____

_____

_____

_____

What subjects do consistently intrigue you?

_____

_____

_____

_____

_____

About what do you have strong opinions or extensive knowledge? Think of the things you could talk about for endless hours with friends, family, and strangers alike.

_____

_____

_____

_____

WORKSHEET

What challenges have you faced, personal experiences have you gotten through?

_____

_____

_____

_____

_____

What do you love? Go crazy on this one because here is where the gems lie.

_____

_____

_____

_____

_____

_____

_____

_____

_____

_____

_____

You are ready for an awakening, a revival of sorts…so, the grand question is

"How can your life reflect all that you desire and are naturally able to create?"

Every day, the sun reassures us it will rise again and bring warmth and growth to all living things on earth, and ultimately, serve its purpose to light the world. Why not consider following its lead?

Each new day is your chance to rise to the occasions your life brings you, to share your warmth in its many forms—compassion, tolerance, acceptance, and to simply radiate. Take advantage of your gifts and plant them in as many places, share them with as many people, as many chances as you are given.

Flowers bloom; they open up their petals from the cool night before to confront the day and be gently swayed by the breeze. They generously offer up their sweet nectar for the honeybees. What sweet nectar does your life, your genius, your art have to offer?

When you say "Yes" to your deep desires, even when you feel scared, and you will be many times, it's important to remind yourself of the amazing adventures and outcomes that await you if you move forward. I am here to evoke something in you that perhaps has been dormant for some time, or perhaps you've yet to discover. It's that magic within you, the one that's never left you.

Here To Shine

WORKSHEET

Just Bust a Move

Share a memory of a time you cleared the dance floor, or dropped some jaws and left some mouths hanging open. I'm sure you have plenty of good moves to talk about. Those moments were your convivial nature in action, in motion. Tap into the spirit of that night, of that moment, and inject it into your life. Just let loose! The world is your dance floor. Revisit and record that moment here. List five opportunities where you can experience something similar and get the process of rekindling your spirit going again.

_____

_____

_____

_____

_____

_____

_____

_____

_____

_____

_____

_____

_____

_____

_____

_____

_____

_____

The Convivial
Woman's Vision

The Convivial Woman exists
to praise and promote human
creativity and the idea that a
work of art resides within you.

My message:

**You are a
Masterpiece.
Live accordingly.**

Convivial Road Map to follow:

Nurture your person

If you focus on discovering what brings you joy, all that makes you come alive; if you take the time to get to know yourself, what you like and don't like, what you want and don't want, then you will create the room to move onto the next phase, which is to...

Ignite the creator

By taking the time for yourself, to explore the world for yourself, you clear the path for the muse to come through to inspire and bring you opportunities to express yourself.

Live the life

Through your conscious efforts to make time for you and say yes to all that nourishes your soul and no to what doesn't serve you, you begin to make time to better express the work of art in you. This state of being puts you in position to design a convivial life all your own and thus fully live it.

These three routes all intersect, coincide, and merge at various points in life, but if genuinely followed they will not conflict or collide.

Using this road map to design your life can help you make choices about how you spend your time, where your energy goes, and how your life can be ultimately experienced.

My words and efforts are not here to preach or declare one kind of convivial creator, how they carry themselves in the world, in their relationships, how they say all the right things and get everything they want if they follow certain guidelines or steps or play the game right.

No, it's about something grander—

It's about Life...

your life—seeing and treating it as you would a work of art and finding a way to creatively express the many versions of you.

It's also about the emotional challenges that each artist faces in this process of self-actualization. We all want to experience freedom and that comes through our desire to create and in our admiration, sharing, and feeling for art... for ourselves.

PART I:
Nurture Your Person

When I was 18, I learned a tough lesson on the emotional perils of not putting myself first. I allowed my desire to please others get in the way of my ability to make a personal and crucial decision to start living my life as I envisioned.

Eighteen…that lovely age when you suddenly feel the world in the palm of your hand and then…dammit, someone comes along and you let them snatch it from you. Believe it or not, many times the said *snatcher* is someone dear to you, someone who loves you.

The Lowdown

My friend Marie and I had been spending a lot of time together, contemplating our futures, having good times and wanting more similar experiences. I can't recall when it happened, but we decided, "Hey! Let's move in together!"

Growing up watching American television, I was brought up to think that moving out of mom and dad's house when you were *of age* was a given. It was so ingrained in my mind that in one journal inscription of mine at 14, I cast myself as an imaginary member of MTV's The Real World in Austin before they ever officially filmed there.

It was simply a part of my mainstream cultural upbringing to think that when the time came for you to become self-sufficient, you went out and tried to figure out this thing called Life. I never got visuals of me fumbling my way through it, so it just seemed like the next best step for me to take.

Marie and I scoped out a few apartments and found a beautiful one near downtown Dallas. It was a neighborhood for up-and-coming, young professionals known as *The Village*. I saw myself that way—I was working, going to school, and had everything ahead of me. Did I know it all? Of course not, but that was the point of embarking on this new journey—to get started learning how to stand on my own in life.

Learning To
Put Yourself
First

I went home with pure joy and all of the possibility in my heart to tell my parents the news. I didn't see it as asking for permission, but more so that I was informing my parents that I'd made a decision. Here's the thing: it was important for me to leave my parent's home on good terms, so I was in no way prepared to have to fight for what I wanted.

I'll never forget that day.

When I shared the news, the one person whose words I remember most were my father's. He said, "You're not ready." And somewhere in there, both my parents tag teamed and said, "It's our wish that you leave our home *married*."

I can't tell you what all was said after that because every word that followed sounded like gibberish to me, but I do remember how I felt. My excitement became muffled. My dream was fading fast. Momentum shut down and I could no longer see the possibility in what I wanted, because now I had to choose between my desire and my parents' desire *for* me, which ultimately translated to their desire.

Being the good daughter I was raised to be (seriously I was TOO good), and knowing all of the heartache and disappointment my parents had already experienced with my sibling, I couldn't see myself going against them. So I chose their way over mine and stayed put. We didn't discuss it again. Only years later would I realize the impact that that decision would have on me and the disappointment I would feel because of it.

Had I gone with what I desired, had I put myself first, had I lived for me in that moment, my only option would have been to rebel, and I was not suppose to be the child who did that in my family. I didn't want to rebel, though. I was not trying to upset anyone; I was simply wanting to be set free into the world, into my own life to discover, explore, and live it for myself. If that meant I had to rebel, then I would have needed to have the strength to "go against" my parents for the sake of creating the momentum I needed to walk my own path. Yet, I didn't have the will to do it at the time.

Culture and belief systems can get in the way of your freedom as they did for me. This happens to so many young women and many times they end up in marriages or with babies at early ages because they are seeking freedom in the wrong way. At what point do they get to feel empowered because they've proved they can handle life without the cushion of someone else?

The strength, will, and desires of so many women combined are, in my opinion, a sleeping giant just waiting for its time to be awakened and shown how life is truly meant to be lived...convivially. I am here to do my part to enlighten the sleeping giant that I believe is the subconscious of women and the men who care for them. The world needs every bit of their talent and energy, if only they can be supported and given the chance to spread their wings and fully realize it.

Convivial Essentials: Be Defiant

Earlier this year, I was up late reading *The Secret Life of Salvador Dali* by the man himself Salvador Dali and I burst into laughter when I came across this passage:

I was twenty-two. I was studying at the School of Fine Arts in Madrid. The desire constantly, systematically and at any cost to do just the opposite of what everybody else did pushed me to extravagances that soon became notorious in artistic circles. In the painting class we had the assignment to paint a Gothic statue of the Virgin directly from a model. Before going out the professor had repeatedly emphasized that we were to paint exactly what we "saw."

Immediately, in a dizzy frenzy of mystification, I went to work furtively painting, in the minutest detail, a pair of scales which I copied out of a catalogue. This time they really believed I was mad. At the end of the week, the professor came to correct and comment on the progress of our work. He stopped in frozen silence before the picture of my scales, while all the students gathered around us.

"Perhaps you see a Virgin like everyone else," I ventured, in a timid voice that was not without firmness. "But I see a pair of scales."

I couldn't help but appreciate this excerpt because it made clear what it means to see the world for yourself. It's just another reminder that everything is perception, and it demonstrates how on any given day, for any task set before you, someone else who believes they know better or best will expect you to follow their lead, see as they see, and act according to their example. But you don't always have to. As a convivial creator, it's up to you to express the vision that lies before your own eyes, to go against the noise, break free from the norm, and embrace the quiet messages guiding you from within.

The True Meaning of Rebellion

If I'd had a better understanding of the word rebellion, I'm certain I would've gone forward with my plans to move out of my parent's home at 18. But I didn't, because I was taught to see rebellion as negative, something to avoid. However, here is how you as a rebel in a convivial world can begin to see it:

Rebellion is...

your refusal to follow or express what doesn't feel true for you.

I came to understand rebellion in this way after considering the turbulent relationship I observed between my parents and my brother growing up. My brother was outgoing, made friends easily, could play almost any sport, drew well enough that DC Comics should've come knocking on his bedroom door, and yet, he was the problem child. He proved to be more than willing to fight anyone's reign over him.

I believe much of his defiance stemmed from our strict religious upbringing. The rules of our church proved to be a hindrance on the very basic need for my brother to be as expressive and expansive as possible. He needed and was eager for as much exposure and opportunities to flex its creative muscles, to communicate his ideas to the world in as many ways his body and hands would allow him. And because that was not being offered to him, he felt the need to break free from the rules and ideas infringing on his personal growth.

It takes courage to stand up for what you want, to speak your mind, to make it very personal, so personal that you are able to put yourself first. Although I would've preferred less heartache for my parents, I still have much admiration for my brother. Unfortunately, it is not always clear to understand people's intentions, but perhaps this story can shed light on how you can keep an open mind.

So, next time you encounter a defiant spirit, whether it be the one within you or another person's, remember that there is a truth beneath that rebellion wanting to be expressed, deserving to be heard.

Be willing to be courageous and genuine, and, if necessary, be rebellious. You never know what changes can come out of your personal acts of conviction.

Follow Your Heart to Find Your Art

I kept journals since age 9. I remember clearly going into a store that could've been the first version of a Dollar store before they became so commonplace. I asked my mother to buy me a diary I saw with a red cover. My first inscription started off this way: *Today I ate eggs and grandma and grandpa are visiting us in Chicago.*

Did my mother tell me, "You know, you should write, so here—here's a diary to start"? No, she didn't. She was busy working two jobs to help my father pay the bills of that 90-year-old brownstone apartment we called home in Chicago.

Something compelled me to grab that diary off the shelf. Something that I was unaware of planted the desire within me to want to write down my thoughts, what I felt, how my days went, who was making a difference in my life and who was giving me hell. I didn't grab the journal from the shelf thinking, "Ooh, I need this to capture my every thought." It was a simple and innocent unconscious desire. It was the muse beckoning me before I even knew what the word "muse" meant.

I wrote in this little book day after day. I got into the business of recording my life in it. I spoke directly to the page as if it were a close friend. I poured my heart onto the blank sheet: I made things up, like getting one of the pages signed by each member of The Bangles. I didn't know the girl's names, so I made them up and signed each of their names differently. Did I ever show anyone this alleged "autograph" I scored at a Bangles concert? No, it was just for fun. It was make-believe. I pretended to have gone to their concert because I had never been to a concert and wanted to create that experience for myself in some imaginary form.

I also wrote about a boy named Ricky, with who I was absolutely infatuated. Inscriptions that went down in that book's history were along the lines of, "I kissed Ricky, then gulped down a huge glass of koolaid!"

Writing was an outlet for self-expression. It was the creative in me letting loose, exploring my world, analyzing it, breaking it down into feelings. That little diary gave me the acceptance, comfort, and unconditional love that I needed to cultivate in myself because the world offers no guarantee of helping you with that task.

Art is healing. It can save you in so many ways. It can serve as your therapist, your saint, a kind of intermediary. And for that reason, it is crucial for you to pay attention to the things and activities that take possession of your spirit and erase all time because that is where you connect to the core of who you are, to the spiritual being and heaven that resides within you. It's your own inner art museum, one in which you have a free pass to visit often.

Trust Your Inner Witness

When I was 15 years old, I transferred to a high school on the outskirts of Chicago and sat in an orientation session for new students. The school's vice principal was discussing the word "vocation" with our group and how it related to the pursuit of our education.

I was intrigued by the word and later looked it up in the library's humongous dictionary (remember those?) and came to understand its meaning very well…

I am alive for the purpose to determine and be engaged with all that summons me to action, what I have a persistent inclination for, and what is continually calling me.

I walked home solo that day and still had the word lingering in my mind. As traffic rolled by, I pondered, "What is my vocation?"

Before I was able to speak, I heard,

"You're a writer."

The answer came through like a shooting star. I was overcome with a sense of calm, like I had figured out something so simple yet profound. No questions or second-guessing followed. Writing was a huge part of my existence, so why shouldn't I fashion my entire world and life around doing it? Most likely, I went home, ignored my chemistry homework, and recorded that moment in my journal.

A few years passed, and I was now a high school senior living in Dallas, Texas. It was my turn to walk across the stage to reach for my diploma, but before that I was given the only senior award for my work as an English student. I never aspired to earn that award and wish I could say I know where it is now, but that was probably life's first attempt to show me that writing was the path I should take.

Like so many, I went down a different rabbit hole. I didn't have the vision, the encouragement, the mentors, the confidence, and I wasn't resourceful enough to pursue my vocation from the get go.

I graduated high school and fell into Banking. Necessity was the reason for many of my initial career decisions. I needed to make money, to pay the $400 balance on my new credit card ('cause back then I thought I was splurging), to pay my car note, keep the insurance man at bay, and most importantly, my college education. It was all up to me.

As a college freshman, I was repeatedly asked what I wanted to pursue as a career, and inside that little voice said, "Writing" but I ignored it. Perhaps, if the question would've been phrased a little differently, something more like, "So, what are you really interested in learning, seeing, doing every day of your life, right now?", I would've been more willing to state what I wanted aloud, and then a dialogue would've opened up about the pros and cons, about the mere possibility in pursuing that desire.

That's what good questions do. They lead to more good questions, thus helping you to funnel your answers and your way to the right course of action. In my case, I would have gone for the journalism or creative writing degree versus a Finance degree.

Your natural strengths, interests, and hobbies are key drivers to get you where you want to be in life, and although you won't always be sure how to invest your time, you can put on your convivial thinking cap and ponder once again the question,

"What are you really interested in learning, seeing, doing every day of your life, right now?"

Let that question be one of many guiding lights to illuminate the path only you are meant to walk. Let no seemingly crazy want or desire go unspoken, unwritten, unshared, unexplored. It exists in you for that very purpose…to be lived.

How much more willing would you be to dip your toes in, or better yet, fully immerse yourself into new experiences if that was the approach you took to living?

When you're in the first decade of your adult life, there is much to figure out. The picture can get fuzzy, yet the voice inside, that inner witness reaching out to you, tugging at your heart, will never be muffled, unless you blatantly ignore it, and honestly, I don't know how possible and true that can be. Perhaps you'll need to ask someone regretful about not following their heart in the many ways they know they should have done so. Ask them if that voice has been silenced in their mind. I know mine hasn't stopped yapping, and I'm thankful.

When deciding on what I would study for a degree plan, there were two reasons I went with Business: a very kind, wise, successful man from Big Spring, Texas told me, "If you aren't sure what you want to do, you can never go wrong getting a Business degree," and because I have a smidgen of realism to me. You must be willing to take risks, to be impractical and defiant in the face of those who so eagerly reject visionary thinking, but there does need to be a balance within you.

In no way do I want to downplay the value of anyone's passion for business because, as it turns out, I later discovered that I was just as passionate about business, the development and creation of it, as I was about writing. And as much as art is about freedom, there is a certain realism that we must juggle in our minds and a constant consideration of what it means to you to live well.

So I continued working in Banking and Finance, fell in love with a man from San Miguel de Allende—a colorful, colonial town in central Mexico. He was high on life and I told him three months after meeting, "I could marry you." And I did just that. After returning from our honeymoon, some kind of switch turned on deep within me. I returned to the States a whole new person. I came back with a new outlook on the world, on how life could be lived, and came to truly understand Oliver Wendell Holmes when he said, *"The mind, once expanded to the dimensions of larger ideas, never returns to its original size."*

Release control and go with the flow

Life is either a daring adventure or nothing.

—Helen Keller

I have my husband and honeymoon to thank for planting the seed of convivial living in me; it gave me the craving to want to quit the world as I'd known it.

I got married one year prior to graduating college (weird timing, I know), and my husband was in charge of planning our honeymoon. He surprised me the day we went to get my passport and the clerk asked me where we were going. Clueless, I glanced toward my soon-to-be hubby and asked, "Where are we going?" He replied, "Tell her you're going to Rome."

Pure elation invaded every cell in my body, translating to a giddy smile, nearly screaming aloud and pulling off my first backflip. But I knew I had nothing on Nadia Comaneci when it came to acrobatics, so I kept my composure and repeated what he said to the lady behind the window.

I couldn't believe it. I soon learned that our plan was to fly into Rome, Italy and fly out of Paris, France. That was it. No further itinerary. The goal was to truly explore the new countries we would set foot on. There would be no hotel check-in upon arrival, no cars or vespas to rent, no four stars to concern ourselves with, none of that.

It was just the two of us flying from one continent to another, and it would be him and I jumping from train to train, venturing from city to city to see what new sights and unique experiences each day would bring. This would prove to be a raw travel experience for us.

I knew my husband was spontaneous, but this seemed over-the-top, fly-by-the-seat-of-your-pants kind of living, and I won't lie and say I wasn't nervous. This experience as well as my husband's seemingly crazy plan to not have a plan taught me to trust in the unknown, to have faith in not having all of the answers up front, to go with the flow.

Life is an adventure with winding, twisting, and sometimes, unpaved roads to unknown destinations.

It requires you to be willing to pack at a moment's notice, throw everything you need into one bag, run through the rain with excitement and a rush of uncertainty, jump into a speeding car, and board the plane that will take you to places you've never been, perhaps you never thought or imagined you'd ever go.

I enjoyed seven cities in Europe during our three-week stay and was able to tuck that journey under my belt and come back with memories of the finest details and 28 rolls of Kodak film in tow. I have no doubt about the altering effect that trip had on my state of being, my psyche, my entire outlook on life and how I wanted to live it. Such moments that come to mind in the most minute ways from that trip are…

Tasting authentic Italian cannoli at a small bakery around the corner from Il Duomo in Florence, Italy. As I bit down onto the pastry's creamy ricotta-filled shell and savored the chocolate chips and pistachio sprinkled throughout, I can say Florence had momentarily become the sweetest spot on earth for me. That town had a magnetizing, hypnotic effect on me. I was in heaven and couldn't place my finger on what did it...

Remembering the first friend of my husband's he introduced me to when we first began dating in Dallas... we bumped into that same friend at the train station in Rome on our honeymoon. He joined us on our walk to The Vatican and spent the rest of the evening with us. After that, I couldn't be more convinced of how small the world really is...

Unexpectedly attending a soccer match between rivals Real Madrid and Valencia, sitting in the area that served as a dividing line between the two team's rival fans, and then speeding off to jump on a train to Paris that night...

Freezing my toes off in Paris with winter temperatures at 4 degrees below zero while leaning in to kiss my husband atop the Eiffel Tower...

Before going to Europe, I thought it to be this grand place, so vast that I couldn't imagine taking in as much as I did in the three-week period that I was there.

Something awoke in me the day...

I ate my first slice of real Italian pizza (with tuna and black olives on it). I was breathing in a new kind of air as I walked the quiet streets of Rome on Christmas day and saw the infamous Coliseum from an alleyway upon stepping out of a local café.

Or when I strolled the city of Venice at six in the morning, hearing nothing but the echo of my husband's and my footsteps, I had to contain my excitement at the first sighting of gondolas docked at their respective piers.

There was an ecstatic force beaming inside of me as I donned myself from head to toe in black wardrobe to walk the alleyways of Florence, Italy.

All of this enlivened me in ways I'd not experienced before. I was physically taking in the world—my body felt it. My mind was living a dream through every sight my eyes glimpsed, every scent I breathed in, every fresh ingredient my palate absorbed. The sounds my ears leaned in for cannot be overlooked; nor can the building corners in which I posed or the statues and articles of clothing I was able to get my hands on.

There were many other moments in Madrid, Barcelona and Paris, but that's for another guide.

A Colorful Town in Mexico

Since I had never been to my husband's home-town of San Miguel de Allende, he included this magical place on the trip itinerary as part of a finale to our honeymoon experience.

Our whole time dating, he bragged about the artsy-fartsy feel of the place and said I would love it. I thought, "Is he just saying that because he's from there?" When we finally arrived and were being driven by taxi into this town nestled in a valley, I was able to glimpse the picturesque city from the high roads we drove down, and my heart started to pound. I could feel excitement building up.

I watched the town locals pass me by and breathed in the smells of the Mexican street vendors' offerings which would become my favorites: tacos de bistec, tortas de milanesa, huaraches, volcanes, and gringas. I felt a huge smile wanting to burst out of me and noticed my husband peeking at me from his rear view mirror as he rode shotgun and directed the taxi driver to his mother's house, but I didn't let him in on my excitement just yet.

I was smitten from the moment I set foot on those cobble-stone streets and walked alongside the colorful, colonial buildings that led me uphill to the heart of San Miguel de Allende, El Jardin. This is the place where every local gathered to get a front row view of the town's magnificent 500+ year-old church, La Parroquia de San Miguel Arc Angel. I was elated to have arrived to such a transcendent place. I was already under its spell, thus proving my husband right all along.

Traveling to these many beautiful and historical places rekindled the convivial nature in me and opened my eyes to all that life had to offer me and anyone else who was willing to say yes to the journey.

In the end, the destination isn't
what matters, it's the experience
made on the journey that does.

You could pair up with any well-traveled person, and both of you can declare having visited the same places, but the individual experiences and the life enhancing effects such places can have on each of you are incomparable. The experience is yours to keep; the memories yours to house in the chambers of your heart forever.

Once your eyes are opened to new possibilities of how to express yourself, how to approach your life, how to solve problems, you'd be defeating and lying to yourself if you ignore implementing that new knowledge into your life.

There was no turning back after this experience. This was the moment when the direction of my life had switched gears, though I was not yet aware of it. The wheels were in motion and I was on my way to a new world, a more convivial one.

The Places that Call You

Leaving the country sparked an interest in me to want to move out of the city where I was living. The unforgettable memories of growing up in the inner city of Chicago played a big factor as well.

I grew up in a neighborhood known as Bucktown, and on my block I played with kids from such distinct ethnic backgrounds as Mexican, Brazilian, Puerto Rican, Polish, and African-American. My brother and I were the Texan transplants. There was a tavern on the corner of our block and we had the option to walk to five other corner stores for snacks and drinks if needed. The culture was simply to be outside hanging out on the fronts steps with your friends or by yourself.

I spent numerous days sitting in front of my apartment building writing in my diary. I took in the sounds of birds chirping, the hum of traffic on the nearby Kennedy Expressway, and enjoyed the cool summer breeze on my face.

Every day was so different, but the one thing that proved to be constant were the faces bound to show up. Back then, I don't recall having all of these expectations of myself, of my writing, from my relationships, of what to make of my life…we just took moments and people in as they came.

The quest to curate a more convivial life is an effort to return to those simpler times, and even though you don't know what the next moment can bring, show up ready for a grand time anyway.

Finding ways to embrace each new day is what I want to encourage you to do in your own world. You will find yourself more relaxed and present and more centered when its time to get something done.

The Path To Convivial Living

Ever want to quit your job? A relationship? A bad habit? A project you no longer feel passionate about? How about a belief that doesn't suit you anymore? If any of the above is not fulfilling you, it's up to you to change it because your happiness and well-being are paramount. However, let me say this: I am not encouraging you to be reckless, careless, thoughtless, and for example, quit a job that pays you and sustains your livelihood because what many would-be artists don't realize until after the fact is that art needs a patron.

You need someone to support the things you truly want to pursue in life, and many times that patron needs to be YOU because as author and educator, Junot Diaz told me this year at a crowded reading in Austin, Texas, "it is an extremely rare thing when someone gets your project, extremely rare." Even if you have the luxury of a spouse who supports you, there is no substitution for making your own money. Now that we're clear on that, let's talk about the best friend you can ever have—intuition.

Intuition will tell you when its time to quit and move onto something new, and if you don't follow the inner compass pointing you in a new direction, guess what happens? You get called in with the rest of the folks you work with for a big announcement by head honcho guy and you get laid off, perhaps even on your birthday. Talk about some gift of divine intervention, huh? That's how life plays out for you when you aren't willing to throw down a hand yourself.

This kind of scenario happens when you ignore the call from the inner witness telling you to make some new moves. Life is more than willing to put you in a position to act, but do you want to be in a position for belly laughs as you look back and say, "Arrivedecci!"? Or do you want to be that person who has to excuse themselves for a good wail because it suddenly hits you that you let it drag on far too long and you're now left with few options?

Help yourself as much as you can. The good news is regardless of how things play out, you'll always find yourself with a new beginning, another chance to do different, learn from mistakes, and live potentially better. Trust that it will all work out because it will.

Convivial Awakenings

Quality of life starts when I can see myself reflected in the eyes of my friends, and the person I see is likable, with dignity. In living the good life, my "I" vanishes, transformed into a real "we"—a "we" made whole by community...

In convivial societies, work is fun, beautiful, and dignified. The schizophrenic separation of work and leisure vanishes. Personal freedoms are only limited when they impinge on another member's equal freedom. This implies communal autonomy—increasing your capacity to self-govern...

—Madhu Suri Prakash, Penn State professor and co-author of Grassroots Post-Modernism: Remaking the Soil of Cultures.

Want to feel that coming-off-the-ground feeling of being alive? What makes *you* feel that way? Do you see yourself in your life? Is there an awakening slowly brewing within you? What are you willing to do about it?

When it comes to creating a change in your life, there's a process you must go through before that change can take full effect. It's an unfolding, an experiment, a personal evolution that you must show up for every day once you make the commitment to reach down into your soul and bring your dreams up for air. It's the act of breathing the life only you can breathe into them.

Changing The Course Of
Your Life Is Possible

When you're at a crossroads in your life—and believe me, you'll find yourself there plenty of times—it's crucial to pay attention to the signs that point you in the direction of where the next treasure awaits you.

When I was a banker, I had the choice of climbing the corporate ladder to figure out my place in the matrix, but there was an inner voice coming through that was causing me to pause and hold back. The more I paid attention to this whisper, the louder and clearer it got.

It was beckoning me to acknowledge, pursue, explore, believe in, and say yes to my passion for writing. By taking that one step, I would learn to embrace every other desire and opportunity life would soon send my way. I was on the verge of an awakening. An epiphany had to occur so I could find comfort and courage in the decisions I would need to make to change direction.

Mine came about after returning from my seven-city tour of Europe. I knew how life could be savored and didn't want to exist only. I heard things like, "Do what you love and the money will follow" and the words haunted me. I began to question everything about my life and felt a change coming. The feeling became so strong, but initially, I didn't know what to do about it.

I was complaining more—"this apartment's too small…I need more closet space…my job sucks." These are the first signs to notice when change is on the horizon. You get agitated and nothing seems to satisfy you.

Frustrated and ready to act, I moved apartments and switched from a job sitting behind a desk to one that had me standing practically all day. Wrong move! I realized that it was time to leave banking altogether. But how would I do that?

When you feel unclear and doubtful on how to transition from one phase of life or one circumstance to another, keep entertaining the thought of what you want to see happen, how you want to feel. The right tools, people, and information will come your way so long as you place yourself in a position to receive it.

One night while flipping through O Magazine, I read a profile on author, Beverly Donofrio who wrote the book-turned-Hollywood cult classic, *Riding in Cars with Boys*. She couldn't find solid ground anywhere, moved a lot, never bought a home until she went to the central Mexican town of San Miguel de Allende. Her picture's caption said: *Beverly Donofrio at her home in San Miguel de Allende.*

Epiphany Struck

I declared, "That's it. I've gotta go," At that point, I knew I was headed for San Miguel de Allende and decided to look for Beverly once I arrived. Beverly said, "If you trust and go for what you want, like a hurricane, the universe pushes open one wharp-stuck door after another and showers you with its gifts." I was ready to begin a new whirlwind story of my own. I was done with being an escape art-ist. No more crying to friends over the phone on lunch breaks about not doing what I loved. I was starting new, starting over.

It's no coincidence San Miguel de Allende was my destination. It had chosen me five years earlier when I met and fell in love with my husband, a town local. I was ready to make the choice to em-bark on a sabbatical to Mexico in order to begin this new story of my life. That meant I would have to be apart from my husband for this experience to become real. Tell me, what woman does that after only two years of marriage? A determined and awakened one.

When you're itching for a change and you listen to the rumbling of your tired soul, you will make choices that baffle everyone around you but make clear sense to you. Go with your gut. It will never fail you.

Resistance

When I felt bold enough to follow my feeling and communicate it, my hubby thought I was crazy. "Quit your job to become a writer?" he asked. A far-fetched idea to him, but it made perfect sense to me. He wanted to know what my plans were upon returning. "I don't know those details yet, but I have to do this. I have to begin *somewhere*," I said.

Girlfriends were saying, "You shouldn't leave your husband alone for so long…" When I gave advance notice of my resignation, my manager tried to entice me to stay with a new part-time schedule and the same pay. With a confident smile, I told him, "Thank you, that's very nice of you, but I gotta say no." He smirked and said, "You know, I did that whole starving artist thing. It's not all its cut out to be." But I wasn't interested in his experience; I was interested in mine, the one that was in the midst of unraveling unknown gems of wisdom to me.

Discouragement translated to gibberish. My mind was unchangeable. When that exit date finally arrived, I quit as planned and headed for Mexico. A new official beginning was underway.

How aware are you of the power you have to change the details of your own life's story? When you find yourself upset, finding every little thing wrong around you, there is something within you that needs to be given an outlet for discussion and expression.

How can you ever know what is worth your attention and effort if you never try it, if you don't listen to yourself, if you let naysayers get the best of what your conscience dictates is true for you? You've got one life to live so claim those experiences for yourself. You have every right to do so.

| Breaking Internal Barriers

My husband and parents accompanied me to San Miguel and my excitement was off the charts once we arrived. Eventually everyone had to leave, except me. Oops, this was for real. I thought, "Holy shit, they're really going back without me." Reality sunk in.

My parents left early and when it was hubby's time I was extremely quiet as he rolled his luggage to the taxi. On the ride to drop him off, I closed my eyes, fighting back tears. I felt like a kindergartner being dropped off at school for the first time. Who were these people I would stay with? What the hell was I doing?

I had left my job, city, country, currency, language, and now my husband was leaving me. I told him I was scared and he kissed me and said, "Everything's gonna be alright." He gave me the strength to say good-bye to him. As he walked to the terminal for boarding, I waved and blew him one last kiss. He was gone and my adventure had begun.

The Subconscious Speaks in Dreams

Dreaming is a common way for your subconscious to communicate with you. It is in dream mode that you're least likely to experience any interference from your rational side—the side that is more than ready to combat all of those crazy choices you may be willing to entertain.

On my first night alone in Mexico, I had a vivid dream…

My husband and parents were with me. In the distance, there was pure darkness. My father mentioned something about a shooting star and pointed upward. In the sky, my mother gestured toward a bright light falling from the sky. I disagreed and said that it looked too big to be a shooting star.

In slow motion, the light, resembling a fireball, was falling fast to the earth. On the horizon, my mother and I saw it touch down. Upon impact, I realized that it was a meteor. When it hit, the impact was exactly as I had seen in big budget Hollywood movies. In that moment, I knew it was the end of the world.

I recalled what all of the scientists and environmentalists had said in earlier days, that the world would end with the impact of a meteor. I saw the build up of energy far away in the distance, and it was fast approaching me. I accepted my fate that I would soon die and found peace about it. I spoke to The One Higher Up, saying, "God thank you for this time on earth. Thank you for the life you let me live." With strength and courage, I looked the explosion directly in the eye and waited to die, yet in that instant as the mass energy was ready to cause my body to disintegrate, instead death seemed to pass me over and immediately, the world before me converted into what looked like a bird´s eye-view of Monterey, California.

I saw all new colorful landscapes—hills, mountains, oceans, trees and clean roads. It looked like Paradise. I was situated in the dream on top of a mountain, looking upon the new earth that now resided beneath my feet. Then, I awoke to my mother-in-law´s bedroom.

I tried to decipher a meaning from that dream and much later, I came to believe that it dealt with the fear I was harboring inside from being in a foreign place. I had left my entire world, the one that was familiar to me in Dallas for San Miguel de Allende. That decision alone was scary, unnerving, and I was filled with doubt about the outcome of my choice. Still, I walked through the doorway of certainty and into the vast unknown, ready to contribute and receive the benefits of the new world awaiting me on the other side.

Follow Your Heart to Find Your Art | Part I: Nurture Your Person

I thought it ironic how I disagreed when my father mentioned that the light in the sky was a shooting star because I knew all along it was not. When I saw the meteor crash to the Earth, fear overwhelmed me, yet immediately passed over me. Without knowing, a new world was given to me because of my release of fear for what the future held for me. I like to believe it was reassurance that the universe was conspiring in my favor, somehow telling me this new world would treat me right, that I would come out okay in the end, that something beautiful would come about as a result of my courage.

With that choice of facing the end of one world and being unexpectedly granted a new, more beautiful one I was on my way to becoming a whole new person, a woman willing to venture from one mystery to another.

When you're taking risks to reach new places, to grow in knowledge and experience, to strengthen who you are, you will face down plenty of meteors in the dark distance. You cannot predict the future, but you also should not live in fear of it. You've got to be willing to peek behind door number two. Or create it yourself.

Confidence will lead the way

Taking uncertain and unknown detours in life takes confidence and as one Pulitzer-prize winning author once told me, "you need to have your ovaries well placed."

You need a well of strength for all the times you're not going to have an answer to the questions in your mind, or for when someone wants to know, "So, what's your plan?...How will you make money doing that?"

I remember the day I walked into Atencion San Miguel, the local newspaper that catered to the ex-pat community in San Miguel de Allende, with the gall to ask to write for them. I was in town to write after all, so I was on the lookout for opportunities.

81

One day while strolling through the Jardin near the Parroquia de San Miguel Arcangel, I stopped to develop some pictures at a nearby camera shop. There was a young woman sitting next to me waiting on her pictures as well. I noticed that she had a badge that said "Reporter" along with the logo for Atencion San Miguel. A light bulb went off in my head and I sparked a conversation with her and told her of my intentions while in town. I confidently asked for some direction from her on how I could make that happen where she worked and she happily referred me to the editor in chief of the paper.

Soon, I was standing in front of the receptionist's desk, waiting for the editor-in-chief to come out and meet with me. A tall English man stepped out and I recall his height feeling a bit daunting to my 5'3" frame, but I looked up with a smile and told him without blinking, pausing or hesitating, "I quit my job in Dallas to come write in Mexico, and I'd like to do it with your paper. I have no professional writing background, but I would like the chance to learn from you and your staff."

Intrigued and perhaps appreciating my candid demeanor (the look on his face said so), he agreed and said, "Come back to speak with Roxanne about where you could be of assistance." With a firm shake of his hand, we said our goodbyes, and I then headed to the nearest internet café where I proceeded to blurt out the exciting news over email to all of my family and friends rooting for me back home. I was tempted to re-enact the Flash Dance audition scene but instead let my fingertips do all the dancing across the keyboard.

With each new bold move I made toward what I wanted, I was slowly but surely starting to believe in this thing called dream manifesting.

No Regrets

For nearly four months, I let the sun's rays and birds singing awaken me. I read several books and officially began my days at noon. I roamed the city of San Miguel de Allende day in and day out. I belly-danced, sat in the Jardin eating my favorite ice cream, helado de guanabana, and attended events with The Author's Sala. I chatted with new friends and relatives while feasting on made from scratch, home-cooked Mexican meals. The pan dulce accompanied by creamy atole de chocolate every night was unforgettable.

Local shop owners became close confidants thanks to conversations had over Paulo Coehlo books and great jewelry pieces. I filled notebooks with my own writing in cafes around town, on rooftops overlooking the city and in the Jardin. I went from rubbing elbows with bankers to mingling with published authors. My Spanish improved and sure enough, I met Beverly Donofrio.

I experienced San Miguel as a foreigner and as a local. I lived a moment and experienced a place where the memory proves to be unfading. Though nothing lasts forever, the beauty comes in sharing the five things I learned and want to pass onto you from such an amazing experience:

- Take risks, constantly
- Fear wants you to run from something that isn't after you.
- You can do anything you put your mind to, really.
- Be bold. Ask for what you want.
- Follow your own path. If it doesn't exist, be courageous enough to create it.

Back To Life...

All good things come to an end and just like that, my sabbatical was over. Upon returning home to Dallas, I felt the responsibility to do something with this new experience. The journey had to continue in some new form and I wanted to find a way to best share the stories that had hitched a ride back home with me.

It was quite an adjustment to be back in the States again. I felt slightly depressed the first two weeks, refused to drive anywhere because I had enjoyed being able to walk everywhere for so long. I knew I'd have to snap out of it and begin making new decisions about where to focus my time and efforts with writing and how I would make money going forward. Whatever it turned out to be, I was committed to seeking experiences that would fan the flames of creativity and keep my soul's fire burning bright

I found myself resistant to wearing the color black and became more aware of my love of the color green. I made choices that led me to anything that intrigued and nurtured my curiosity. One such choice was a workshop I attended to learn more about the ancient medicine known as Ayurveda. I'd never read any books about it, known anyone who practiced it, yet something in me was curious to check it out.

Halfway through the workshop, the instructor brought up the importance of utilizing your talents, and a woman in her late 40's raised her hand and asked, "But what if you don't know what your talents are?" My heart sank for that woman. I wanted to give her a hug because I realized that my talent was at age 15, though I was barely getting the process started to develop it in my late 20's, but, for a middle-aged woman to feel she had no understanding of what her unique gifts were…well, it simply broke my heart.

Not knowing is not something to be ashamed of, but it is something to acknowledge and begin taking steps to discover. You could do this by taking up a new hobby, enrolling in a class on a subject that intrigues you, or by traveling. Simply getting out into the world awakens your senses. What are those areas of interest for you? Where are those places into which you wish to venture?

We all feel we need to make sure our time is well spent while alive and there is a purpose to everything we do, but remember to seek experiences, learn new skills, and educate yourself on subjects as a simple escape, an outlet, because there is no end result except to nurture the curiosity in you.

Focus On Sharing Your Lessons

> ## When You're Going Through Hell, Keep Going.
>
> —Winston Churchill

When I was previously going through the emotional rollercoaster of waking up everyday to a job I was no longer passionate about, I wasn't the best company. I did my best to keep my true feelings silent for the sake of others. I didn't want to contaminate anyone's experience with the dissatisfaction I felt for my life, but that act was not possible to keep up.

You either stay silent and slowly go catatonic, or you speak up and get moving, get dreaming, and get creating.

When things are bad, and they don't seem like they can get any worse, and then they do, consider doing these 5 things:

1. Find a confidant who has been there and understands the situation and spill the beans, get their take.

2. Channel Tina Fey. Ever notice how comedians seem to talk about how bad they had it growing up? Sarah Silverman peed her pants a lot, and not when she was a baby. Tracy Morgan wasn't on speaking terms with his mother when his best-selling book came out. Amy Poehler recently broke off her marriage of nine years. How do you think these folks get through the pain? They crack a joke. They don't hide from the facts, but instead bring them all front and center and poke fun at them, one by one.

3. Ride The Wave—when you continually resist the tides that flow in and crash into you, that doesn't stop the tide from returning does it? Why not just immerse yourself in the water, accept that you're getting wet, that this is an uncomfortable moment and have faith that the waves will calm down, the tide will recede, and this will be yet another moment in your life that will pass.

4. Get out of your house slippers—even if they have Donald Trump's name on them—and kick your own ass back into shape. Tough love, baby…we all need it, and if no one's around to offer it, sometimes you've just got to play that role for yourself and heed the words of Bob Newhart and just STOP IT.

5. Gather Your Army—surround yourself with people who know you best, who expect nothing more from you than to just be still and be you. They can help recharge your spirits.

You create every experience in your life, whether good or bad. You have the power and absolute right to say yes or no to whatever comes your way. Some situations will suit you, enhance your way of life, and others won't. To know how to decipher between them is to know what you want for your life.

So, make a move—any move—to get yourself out of unsatisfying situations, and find ways to reverse any negative feelings that may haunt you. There's no excuse to remain immobile, unhappy, and to not do better for yourself and your life. Polish off those brass ovaries, or as my one-time business mentor Marie Forleo said, "get a set," and get to work on a new story for you.

Steve Jobs and The Calligraphy Class

In his commencement speech to Stanford graduates in 2005, Steve Jobs' shared the story of how he briefly attended Reed College in Portland, Oregon and decided against a traditional college education and withdrew from his courses. Then, he stuck around Reed for another 18 months to study calligraphy. Who does that?

Just when you think there's no point to pursuing random interests if there's no purpose or payoff in sight, there is one. In his 2005 speech, Jobs shared these details about his time in that calligraphy class and what came of it…

"I learned about serif and sans serif typefaces, about varying the amount of space between different letter combinations, about what makes great typography great. It was beautiful, historical, artistically subtle in a way that science can't capture…When we were designing the first Macintosh computer, it all came back to me. And we designed it all into the Mac. It was the first computer with beautiful typography. If I had never dropped in on that single course in college, the Mac would have never had multiple typefaces or proportionally spaced fonts. And since Windows just copied the Mac, it's likely that no personal computer would have them."

He took calligraphy because it intrigued him. He had no idea how it would serve him or others but he showed up for class anyway. He took in the information, had no preconceived notions of how

to transfer the knowledge over to his real life…
but later, way later, it all came together.

How can you do something similar?

To start, you can pay attention to:

- What you excel at
- What people often ask your advice on
- What you enjoy doing and how quickly
  the time passes
- What you could read about, learn more
  of, watch many shows on, and talk about
  without losing interest

And then you could even reach out to your family
and friends and ask them what they think you're
good at. You'll see how the ideas begin to pour
in. Most importantly, let your curiosity guide you.
Don't think too much into it. Just follow it. The
more aware you become, the more clear the path
you will see to the things you enjoy and the more
you will be able to contribute and serve.

Art is the vehicle in which you express the creator
in you. Through the sharing of that art, you do
your part to further nourish the world. Whether
you're creating a book, a blog, a necklace, a cake,
a lesson plan, a baby, a new life or body for yourself, or even a meal for your family, if you're heart
is in it, then it is bound to be art worth admiring.

Clarity of purpose, of vision, of yourself makes
you an unstoppable force. Know your power; live
your life indeed, for you are a masterpiece and
should live accordingly. This is the message of a
persistent and generous muse brought to me on
many occasions and which I now bring to you.

Declare and Debut Your Talents

What's your art form? Are you ready to debut your talents, to begin developing them? Let the journey begin by declaring your talents, interests, and passions here.

_____

_____

_____

_____

_____

_____

_____

_____

_____

_____

_____

_____

_____

_____

_____

_____

_____

_____

_____

_____

_____

A Convivial Mindset

A friend once told me, "You know…you're some-one who requires a lot of answers." And it's true. When the details of a friend's story aren't grant-ing me enough of a visual to make their experi-ence come alive in my own mind, I jokingly say, "Put me there!"

Questioning is necessary because it's a way of at-tempting to experience and understand life from as many points of view as possible. You multiply your understanding through the amount of ad-ditional perspectives you're willing to try to see it through. One camera's lens doesn't guarantee the best exposure every time.

My inquiries (not to be mistaken for interroga-tion) give me the chance to walk in another person's shoes. By actively listening to another person share their experience, you can learn new ways to express yourself, how to lighten up or hunker down, perhaps what to avoid altogether and you become that much more evolved as a person in that one moment of conscious connec-tion with another.

When you're willing to dig deep for meaning, to uncover an understanding to life's puzzling mo-ments and continually arising conflicts, whether they be yours or another's, what you're doing is exercising and strengthening your ability to craft better solutions to problems, tell better stories, acquire and pass on lessons learned, and create more positive outcomes for yourself in life.

[Decide what experiences bring out your convivial nature]

PART II:
IGNITE THE
CREATOR

Being self-aware is key to tapping into the emotions and intuition that can guide and steer you through life. How can you gain more self-awareness?

Go do things.

Take on a new hobby. Travel to places you've always dreamed of going. Cultivate yourself, your interests, your life. Make the effort to turn new connections into solid relationships. Explore a subject you've always been curious about. Read the biography of a person who has always fascinated you. You just might find some detail in their story that makes you more aware of your own life, thus validating your initial attraction to that person.

Go do…

is a repeated refrain in the aptly titled song by Jonsi, the guitarist and vocalist for the Icelandic post-rock band Sigur Rós. Here's your glimpse into portions of this powerful song…

Self-
awareness
is key

Go sing, do loud
Make your voice break- Sing it out
Go scream, do shout
Make an earthquake...

We should always know that we can do anything new

Go drum, do go out
Make your hands ache - Play it out

We should always know that we can do everything

Go do, you'll know how to
Just let yourself, fall into landslide

Go do, you'll know how to
Just let yourself, give into low tide

Go do!

We should always know that we can do anything

Go do!

If Jonsi, a man who has only one fully functioning eye, can go do, who or what is stopping you?

Not sure of what you want to go do? Start by paying close attention to those seemingly vague notions that pull your attention in one direction. Like the book about natural cures that catches your attention…at a time when your body's ailing you. Or the book about high infertility rates among women that you throw in the shopping cart because it was $1…the one that turned out to be a page turner for you, thus convincing you to get your baby making on.

I firmly believe that is the muse working to lay down the pavement for you to walk a new path, experience a new something, to make any lingering decision whose time has finally come.

The Imaginary Beacon

When I was a senior in college, several of my final courses were in the same building where many of the liberal arts courses were held. I was taking Money & Banking and Cost Accounting at the time. On bathroom breaks, I couldn't help noticing the bulletin board situated outside a Creative Writing professor's door. I never saw anyone in the office and the door was always locked (yes, I tried turning the knob once). Why did I do that? Something in me *wanted* in.

Upon discovery of this bulletin board, I began to stop by after each escape from class. I would comb the many pinned-up flyers advertising creative writing conferences, contests, and I always grabbed a copy of the newest edition of Writer's Chronicle.

This was a whole other world, so different from the one where I was currently. By day, I was a professional banker, by night, a Finance major, but somewhere buried away was the real me…I was a writer who lost her way. While I was busy working a graphing calculator and solving bizarre matrices and financial equations, I was entertaining a little voice in the back of my head that wanted to know what the hell was I doing and how was any of this calculus really going to serve me in life.

Something kept luring me to that bulletin board, telling me, "Come here…come on in…we've been waiting for you." Yet, I was busy fulfilling the commitments I'd already made and wanted to see them through.

Weeks after walking the stage with my husband and graduating with a *Finance* degree, I decided to inquire about enrolling in the graduate program for Liberal Arts at my same university. I was initially rejected because I lacked sufficient credit courses in the undergraduate English program. Well duh, I was a Finance major doing a complete 180 here and finally giving into my heart's yearning! I was bummed, but undeterred. That was too lame of a reason to close the door on me, so what did I do?

I went back to the doorway of the infamous bulletin board, got the name of the professor and soon, I was sitting in to observe his Creative Writing class and informed him of my pending dilemma. Now, this man didn't know who I was, had no reason to help me, but he did and it worked.

I was accepted and felt pure elation.

How did that happen? Will. Determination. Conviction. Effort. Perseverance. Not taking no for an answer.

The professor saw something in me that resulted in an action he took on my behalf. I am ever grateful for his generosity. I ended up taking my first two graduate courses, felt completely out of place, didn't understand the language of this world, but I was there. My love and interest in writing lured me to the bulletin board; will, creativity, perseverance and the generosity of another person helped get me into class.

This is how a convivial creator must approach obstacles because there will always be some pebble to stumble upon, attempting to hinder you. It's up to you to come up with the fancy footwork to get around it and reach your goal.

> When you do things from your soul, you feel a river moving in you, a joy.

—Rumi

Tap Into All
That Lures
You

If you were to bring up the subject of Dance, I would tell you about my desire to learn these particular forms: Ballet, Flamenco, and Belly dancing. I would then proceed to tell you that each different art form has a deeper meaning for me. Or so I believe.

In pursuing Ballet, I am tapping into a memory that brings me happiness. During my senior year of high school, I got a sampling of ballet during a general dance class I took. I remember my body feeling challenged, yet excited by this art form and then…it was over. We moved onto the next dance. Since then, I've held a curiosity, a craving for more, but have yet to act on it.

Flamenco has a flare to it, an attitude, and there is something in me wanting to express this same attitude. Through the stomping and fierce hand movements of flamenco, is it possible for me to learn to embrace and fully embody the fierce nature that has been passed onto me from my 4'11" mama and grandfather of similar stature? Or could it be the Spaniard blood running through my veins thanks to my lovable father with a name that means King? I won't know until I engage in a class.

Belly dancing also serves to rekindle a moment in my life. When I spent those four months in Mexico, I took a belly dancing class with a woman named Flor. She was sensual and beautiful, which is how this form of dance makes me feel. She had this bohemian look to her, showing up to class with combat boots, a long flowing skirt and her hair pulled up and wrapped with a sash. She was confident when looking at herself in the mirror, moving her waist, and I wanted to emulate that energy as well. It doesn't hurt to know that this dance is based on movements that come naturally to the female body.

Curiosity Trumps Results

There doesn't have to be a result from every activity you pursue. What it boils down to is your curiosity, like when you were a baby swaying your fingers in front of your eyes and learning how to move them one by one.

What activities conjure up good memories for you?

What interests do you have that feel short-lived?

Perhaps its time for a return to innocence.

There's no room to be bored, to wait for another to make plans for you. It's up to you to make plans for yourself and push the boundaries on the experiences you can claim all your own.

Your Convivial Life List

Through engagement comes self-awareness and all that is waiting and ready to be expressed in you.

Dedicate this moment to creating your Convivial Life List.

List 10 things you want to do just because.

_____

_____

_____

_____

_____

_____

_____

_____

_____

_____

_____

_____

_____

_____

_____

_____

WORKSHEET

Now that you have them down, share *why* or what you think is calling them to be part of your top ten? You may find out there's something deeper than just pure interest and curiosity.

_____

_____

_____

_____

_____

_____

_____

_____

_____

_____

_____

_____

_____

_____

_____

_____

Accountability Partners

It's one thing to dream; it's another thing to hold yourself accountable to your word. The thing is, we are more willing to let ourselves down, to slack off when no ones watching or checking in on us, but we're less likely to disappoint another person whose in on the journey with us.

Your job now is to share your Convivial Life List. Go for friends with whom you feel comfortable talking about your wildest dreams AND who are self-activators, people who get shit done in their own life. This list is not for the friend who will politely smile, nod and never bring the subject up again.

So, who is it going to be?

_____

_____

_____

_____

_____

_____

_____

Make a call and make a pact. Ask them to hold you to your word, to your desires and offer to do the same for them. Encourage them to create their own list and check off experiences with you. Make it fun. Find ways to celebrate your accomplishments combined.

Create a reminder on your phone or your calendar to follow up once a week or every month with one another. If you're both local, make it a lunch date. If not, hang out on Skype. Be a team; track one another's progress. Be fully committed to one another.

Reflect

Once you've taken on that new challenge, what's next? It's time to go within and reflect on what you've experienced. We all have a way of processing what we're experiencing, how we express our joy and confusion about life. What's your way?

The goal is to become more in-tune with yourself, more conscious and aware of your wants, and though you may not have all the answers on the road ahead, or even know which way to go, you learn to choose the route and base the maneuvers and turns on intuition.

Sitting idle is not going to bring about any epiphanies. The more clear you are on what is unwanted, the easier you recognize what you do desire and trust in all that calls and guides you toward that want.

WORKSHEET

Take a Trip Back to You

The art of convivial living is a matter of playing in the world as you did as a child—without fear, without inhibition, without worry of what people think of you, without hesitation to simply be who you are.

What are some experiences that bring out that playful, childlike sense in you? What are the memories associated with your inner child? What emotions do they spark? Who brings that essence out in you, how often do you make time to engage?

Without taking a moment to understand these things about yourself, to know where the power within you originates, you may find it hard to draw on your senses and follow up with a creative act that is all your own.

Return to innocence and share your findings here.

_____

_____

_____

_____

_____

_____

_____

_____

_____

_____

_____

_____

_____

Big D and The Three R's

When my family moved to Dallas, I was 16 years old and immediately noticed the wide, empty streets and clean, cookie-cutter neighborhoods with no people out in front of them. Where was the life, the sounds of kids playing in the street? I passed parks and saw empty basketball courts, the swings silent and still. Something about that visual didn't sit well with me. It just didn't feel natural.

I came to learn that Dallas was a great place to get busy. There wasn't much to the city. As a local friend and mentor once said, "Dallas is the three R's: Roads, Retail, and Restaurants." There would prove to be no better way to describe the culture and lifestyle I came to know there.

From the beginning, I felt something missing in this new place my parents declared my new home. I couldn't put my finger on it, but the feeling never subsided. I got busy with college and work. I had every reason to be happy there—I had my parents and one sibling nearby, and I met my husband and had great friends to keep me company and offer support. As an unsuspecting convivial woman at the time, I had plenty of dining options, but where were the vistas, the natural landscapes for me to connect and commune with? I wasn't much for shopping, so the malls on nearly every corner rarely got a visit from me.

When I'd return to Chicago, I was reminded of what life was all about—getting out and enjoying the world, the people around you, playing, walking, running. The same thing would happen when I visited San Francisco, Austin, various towns in Mexico, and I would always return to Dallas with this feeling deep inside telling me, "This isn't it for you; you're not home yet."

After my honeymoon, I knew Dallas wasn't where I wanted to permanently hang my hat. I pointed out all of the details that I felt were missing to my husband. I mentioned the experiences I wanted our future children to have and how I couldn't see it happening where we were. I wanted walkability for them, not to be driven in a car everywhere, all the time.

There was something calling me elsewhere. I wanted to leave, tried to convince my husband to pack his bags with me, but he was settled, comfortable, unwilling to go. I didn't understand it, and I was frustrated. My husband and I had conflicts over the matter and he would tell me, "It's not the city. You just need to change your thoughts about it." Maybe he was right, I thought. Something was aching in me for a change of scenery, but maybe, just maybe he was right and I was wrong. But feelings never lie…

We had travelled to San Miguel de Allende for two weeks and I remember feeling quiet during my stay there. My friend, Marta who lived there noticed and asked "Que trais? Te ves muy diferente, amiga…que te pasa?" She wanted to know what was up with me, even mentioned that I looked very different. She would know the difference because it was only one year prior to that that she witnessed my lively spirit as I spent many days during my sabbatical chatting with her in her shop.

I played it off and told her I was fine, but there was a big surrender coming. I knew it. Once we returned from vacation, I recall driving past the downtown Dallas skyline and began to pray as I glimpsed the lit up buildings, "God help me to accept this city as my home, help me to make my life here and find happiness, help me to experience the joy of being here…"

What I was actually asking for was to replace my desire for another desire that was not my own. Tell me if you think that ever works out the way you want it to? I tried to convince myself, "Hey, if Mark Cuban can make it here, I can too!" I bought a house with my husband and when time came to get the keys to our new house and shake the neighbors hands, I was indifferent. I forced a smile, didn't want to interact. It took me a year to begin decorating my home. I had no desire to re-model anything, enhance anything. In my mind, it was a future rental home, nothing more. I didn't allow myself to get attached.

I'd visited a friend prior to that in Chicago and now had my six-month-old baby boy with me and I still felt that feeling inside, telling me there was somewhere else for me and my family. I had made it clear to my husband that I didn't want my children to grow up in Dallas; I wanted a different experience for them, something closer to how my husband and I grew up. But my husband was indifferent and comfortable. He was content where he was and couldn't see my unhappiness.

I was sitting in my girlfriend's kitchen as she prepared her famous chicken tacos and told her how I was still feeling after all these years. I had the house, the dogs, the great big backyard, the life-loving husband, the baby, my parents were around the corner, and yet, I was still unfulfilled with where I was making my life. She said, "You've been feeling like that for a long time, Cheryl… you really gotta do something about it."

I flew back home with my son and decided I wanted to test something out. I would be picked up from the airport and upon pulling up to the driveway of my house, I wanted to see if I got that feeling of "Ahhh, I'm home." It was night time, and as we drove up to the house, I did my best to put any thoughts out of my head so I could leave room for nothing but the feeling in my body to communicate what I needed to hear. Sure enough, I felt emptiness, a void.

Three years later, I had a friend come to Dallas who was considering moving there. I was his guide and took him around to every part of the city where he could consider living. Deep inside, I felt a bottleneck in my throat, like I wanted to scream,

"Don't live here!" I didn't want to influence his decision or impose my personal thoughts about the town on him because perhaps Dallas could work for him and it was only my issue. But after a few hours of driving, he said, "This city's very vanilla. I don't get any kind of vibe here." When he spoke those words, it was as if he'd found the key to the imaginary shackles on my feet and had taken them off of me. Gleefully, I rejoiced, "I thought I was the only one who thought and felt that!" From that point on, I poured my heart out to him and let him know my experience and it was then that I realized that I could no longer repress my feelings. I knew it was not just me who felt that way, and it was time to recognize that something had to change.

I needed to make my life somewhere else. I knew a battle would ensue with my husband because there was no reason, in his mind, to pick up and leave all we had. But I had a reason, a reason that had been put on the backburner years before and was now boiling over. It was a pressing matter.

I knew opening this can of worms again would bring discomfort and conflict. I anticipated my husband getting upset and possibly saying, "I thought this discussion was over." I knew he would think I was crazy and unrealistic, but I also knew the life in me would die little by little the more I put it off, the more I ignored it. I didn't like the taste of regret in my mouth, so it was time to speak up. The vision I had of life for myself and for my family was dependent on me standing firm and declaring what was important to me, what I couldn't help feeling for so long.

You must remember that the timing of your dreams largely depends on you. The factors outside of your control are most times minor compared to the courageous actions you will be required to take.

In previous years, I wanted to move to San Francisco, or back to Chicago, perhaps even Boston, but now that I had a son, I didn't want to be too far from family. I knew what it felt like growing up without extended family around me and didn't want that for my kids. I thought long and hard about the state of Texas and knew that if I was to stay in the state where my family resided, the only place that called to me was Austin. I can't explain it, but every drive there, every opportunity passing by on I-35 as we headed to Mexico, I felt something luring me there.

As expected, my husband was annoyed when I brought up my desire to move again. He refused to listen, but I knew I would have to be persistent and keep focused on my vision.

This wasn't a selfish act on my part. I understood that change doesn't come easy for everyone and I thought about all of the potential benefits our whole family would reap from the move. Undoubtedly, the positives outweighed the negatives. There were plenty of battles, even one night that I cried myself to sleep. When the morning came, I sat down at the breakfast table as if in a trance and stared out toward my backyard.

At the time, I had just begun my adventures as The Convivial Woman and was prancing around online with the intention to empower women and spread my personal mantra:

Know your power, live your life.

The idea was if you know and believe in the greatness that resides in you and you consciously tap into that powerhouse of strength and will, only then can you truly embody your life.

"The brick walls are there for a reason. The brick walls are not there to keep us out. The brick walls are there to give us a chance to show how badly we want something. Because the brick walls are there to stop the people who don't want it badly enough. They're there to stop the other people.

—Randy Pausch, The Last Lecture

I was faced with a choice in this matter; I could surrender yet again and convince myself that I didn't feel what I felt, that I didn't need or want what I wanted, and I would have to make the best of my circumstances versus creating new ones that reflected what I truly wanted and believe about life. A healer I frequented for Maya Abdominal Massage once told me, "You have a lot of integrity in your body." That was why I was unable to lose myself as a result of putting one of the longest lingering desires within my heart aside.

As my husband sat in front of me eating his breakfast, occasionally glancing my way, wondering what I was thinking, I thought...

If I surrender my desire yet again, I risk a slow death. I will be a hypocrite preaching the message of "Know your power, live your life"...I won't be exercising my own power...I will allow another person's desire for comfort to get in the way of what my heart tells me is true and necessary. I won't be real with myself if I allow this to happen again. And anyone who is willing to stand in the way of my happiness is not thinking of me, but of themselves.

Tears flowed down my face as I pondered giving in when I didn't need to, when I mustn't. I needed to exercise strength and courage to decide to stand firm in what I wanted. I thought, It's all or nothing...Austin or bust. As risky as it could be, I had to accept that this decision could jeopardize my marriage. That wasn't my desire or intention, but if that would be the result of my attempt to be true to me, then I had to be willing to keep my eyes fixed on the light at the end of this seemingly dark tunnel to find out.

There comes a time in your life when you have to make the choice to listen to that voice inside guiding you toward the life you can clearly see yourself living.

Many people choose the route of sacrificing bits and pieces of themselves, day by day, for the sake of not wanting to rock the boat, but is that the choice you want to make? I don't believe it is. It's up to you to believe it, as well.

Three years later, I am happy to say that my family and I live in Austin, Texas and couldn't feel more at home.

My husband is just as happy and appreciates the new challenges it brings his own life. We are all growing as a result and there are no regrets. The heart never lies, and your inner guide never steers you wrong so long as you trust in it to get you there.

Dr. Wayne Dyer once said, "Where there's a will, there's a relative." The people who have the potential to stop you in your tracks are the ones who love and want the best for you. They don't mean to get in your way, but you must prove to them how strong your will and pursuit of personal happiness means through the actions you take, even if it means going against them.

PART III:
Live The Life—A Convivial Life

Once having traversed the threshold, the hero moves in a dream landscape of curiously fluid, ambiguous forms, where he must survive a succession of trials...this is a favorite phase of the myth adventure...it may be that he here discovers for the first time that there is a benign power everywhere supporting him in his superhuman passage...and... is attended by a host of invisible familiars.

—Joseph Campbell, The Hero
With a Thousand Faces

Initiate Yourself

You can read as many books on a subject that fascinates you, talk all you want about the life experiences you crave, or continue wishing for the time you need to develop and master that one true gift of yours, but if you don't get out there and get started now, you won't ever know the future that life wants to reveal to you.

In early 2012, I attended Austin's SXSW conference upon first moving to the Live Music Capitol of the World and walked into the AT&T Blogger's lounge with a couple folks I'd recently met. To my surprise, the author, Hugh McCleod of the highly successful blog, Gaping Void was there signing and giving away copies of his newest book, Freedom Is Blogging In Your Underwear.

I was ecstatic about meeting him because only weeks before that I'd devoured his book, Ignore Everyone & 39 Other Keys To Creativity, in one sitting and fell madly in love with his brain. My turn came to get a picture and book signed by the man, and I paused to ask him about a point he made in his book Ignore Everyone about the need to have a day job outside of your art, to have something to sustain you while you worked to master your gifts. I wanted to know more about his thoughts on my particular path and shared how I struggled with deciding whether I agreed with him. He made me laugh when he said, "I don't know what to tell you! I figured it out for myself, now you go do it!"

When you set out on your own journey, the road can be long and full of worry and doubt. You don't know what you're doing half the time. You feel vulnerable, and when in that state of mind you can either be powerful or extremely weak. It's important to catch yourself when you're on the weak end. When you find yourself seeking answers everywhere except within you; this is the moment to stop, quiet down, and remember that you are the one in charge. You know what is best for you, you really do know which way to go. Fear is the culprit behind your foggy vision and each roadblock you encounter, nothing else. You remain behind the wheel and always have the final say on what happens next.

WORKSHEET

Curating Your World

My ability to begin anew in another city sparks a sense of adventure in me. I wonder, What stores will I discover, what new restaurants will become my go to places for comfort food and good times, what landmarks and parks can I enjoy. But what if moving altogether isn't what your heart craves or may not be feasible?

What are some alternatives to giving yourself the chance to explore what is brewing within you with all that is currently around you?

_____

_____

_____

_____

_____

_____

_____

_____

_____

_____

_____

_____

_____

_____

_____

WORKSHEET

Is there a boutique you've been meaning to pop into, a coffee shop or bookstore that seems to always catch your eye on the drive home from work? Have you read about a great hotel in the city that all the tourists flock to? Why not make a commitment to visit these places and declare yourself on evening or weekend sabbatical?

Make a list of all the potential places you can go to that could give you a strong creative vibe and make you feel as if you're somewhere else. When do you want to go? Set a date, invite a friend or go solo. Give yourself this time to bask in just being you and learn the ins and outs of your town. I guarantee a convivial time.

_____

_____

_____

_____

_____

_____

_____

_____

_____

_____

_____

_____

_____

_____

_____

A Time To Gather

When I first arrived to Austin, I felt this sense of relief. My desire to move was now my everyday reality; I could now call this town home. I had this sense of calm within me. I was able to sleep through the night because I didn't feel the need to be anywhere any more.

The mind can get muddied with the maintenance and messiness of everyday living, and it's in those moments when you just need to breathe and give it time.

There were many days this year when I felt I was neglecting to express myself online as The Convivial Woman. At times, I felt unproductive, like I wasn't accomplishing much, but then it hit me that I have been in the midst of a huge undertaking.

I was creating a new life in Austin for my family and getting myself acquainted and reestablished.

It's not realistic to expect to be creative all the time, to be producing nonstop. There have to be periods of rest, moments of surrender, stages of gathering. When life is happening all around you and you feel you can't take time out for you, it's important to recognize this as a period of absorption. It's a time to take in your next phase of life and the material, lessons, and insights it wants to bring.

Embrace these periods of observation and contemplation, then bring your findings, lessons, insights and epiphanies back to the drawing board and create something straight from the recesses of your rejuvenated and relaxed mind or trust that you'll find ways to incorporate them into your daily life.

A Natural Desire To Show And Tell

> "Every child you encounter is a divine appointment."

—Wess Stafford, President,
Compassion International

It is a grand privilege to witness the beauty and joy of my sons discovering their world, giving new things a try every single day, and wanting everyone around them to recognize and notice what they are accomplishing.

They aren't shy to say, "Look what I did!" They are quick to glance your way when they finish a puzzle, complete their ABC's or simply use the potty for the first time. Every day, there is something new for them to show and tell, to make known to the next person about what they've experienced or acquired in new knowledge. They have no fear because they put no thought into it.

The line *"follow your heart"* has no significance for children. They are so close to the center of who they are that it proves to be easy for them to jump right into whichever creative act is calling their attention at the moment. It's all about the experience, not kudos. The kudos come as a result, but aren't the motivation.

WORKSHEET

Study A True Original

Study your child or nieces, nephews, friend's children (with their permission, of course) for this assignment. Your task is to observe and ponder a child's joy; their words, questions, energy; their fearless behavior and excitement over the most simplest of things. Report back your observations and what activities you think can bring that same spirit out in you.

What experiences can help you return to innocence and bring about more convivial sensations to your life?

_____

_____

_____

_____

_____

_____

_____

_____

_____

_____

_____

_____

_____

_____

_____

A Room For Two, The Muse + You

There are many correlations with spirituality and creativity. I'd never thought to consider the feeling of peace and freedom that comes with practicing art (read: consciousness). When you grab a pen and release your worries, questions, ponderings, and musings to a blank page, or however you express yourself creatively, the feeling it brings can be similar to the act of getting down on both knees, bowing head, clasping hands together and *letting go and letting God.*

That is how the creative process seems to work. In order to create, you must show up so you can immerse yourself to lose yourself. This is the only way to truly connect to that power source within you and feel what is waiting to be created by you.

There is only room for two in that moment: you and the muse. Keep your thoughts about it as simple as possible and simply show up for the moment to get work done. The point is to connect and step into that sacred space with a lot of intention, faith, and allow things to unfold as they will.

As a writer, I experience all sorts of emotional resistance and plenty of excuses when its time to write, but I push through the mind- boggling gibberish to get words down anyway. What I'm aspiring to arrive at is a momentary glimpse of clarity and break on through to experience that lightweight feeling in my body that I always get after making time to express myself. Devote yourself to this same state of bliss.

The Importance of
Creating Space

You can't get convivial if you don't have the space for it.

That sounds a little frisky, but what I mean is, you can't begin to think of creating anything if you're not already dwelling in an enthusiastic and expansive state of mind or physical space.

As some of my revolutionary college friends used to say, let me *break down* this word for a moment (via TheFreeDictionary.com)…

Dwell

to live; reside; to originate (in); to fasten one's attention, to rest in, to exist in a given state or place.

These were the phrases that stood out to me, because when it comes to creativity, you need space to create.

You need it in your head.

You need it in your heart.

You need it in your home.

If you do not make room or maintain space within each of those places, your creativity suffers. I know this all too well.

In your head…

Do you deal with compulsive thinking? This comes in the form of all the worrying you do late into the night, wanting to maintain control all the time, comparing yourself to others, worrying about what others think of you, about what you don't have, about the gifts and talents you don't possess or haven't mastered, about that last piece of chocolate you ate that you didn't need to eat, and there is only one thing any of this will do: bring you down, and guess what? Keep you down.

Focusing on a problem, a weakness, what is missing, what you've yet to "get" only amplifies the issue, delays progress, and weakens you. I'm not saying don't acknowledge your problems, but instead place your attention on how to resolve, alleviate, or completely be done with them. Creativity is a form of seeking solutions, especially when they aren't as evident or in your face.

In your heart…

Is there anyone to forgive in your life? Do you have problems with your sweetheart? Are there relationships you need to part with? Things you need to accept about yourself, your life, past choices you've made and can't change? Forgiveness is the key that unlocks the doorway to a whole heart.

Focus on the activities and people that give you strength and make you feel expansive and proud to be you. The things you cannot change…let them go. Forgive yourself for your mistakes and character flaws. Allow yourself to be human and vulnerable. The world will appreciate your humility and willingness to share your story with them.

In your home…

I still want to believe that it's important to have a space to claim as your own, but I haven't had an office space or a select writing spot in my home for a couple of years now. Just as soon as I had decorated and picked out all the right furniture pieces for my office, my children were born and that space was converted into a family TV room/play area. Can you say chaotic setup for any creative solace? YES.

I was never able to get work done there, so I've since been hopping around from café to café, from backyard lawn chair to kitchen table to living room couch to jotting down notes in my iPhone under the covers at bed time.

These are the ways I've been able to get work done, make progress, and continually grow. I hope to get that space back soon, but for now, it's important to at least be organized and know where work-related things can be easily found and stored.

What organizational systems do you have in place to clear the path to creating?

Most times, getting started with something creative comes out of nowhere and you've got to grab the first piece of scrap paper and pen that is nearby.

If you've got a smart phone and never leave home without it, then you're probably like me, madly typing away your ideas and insights into iPhone Notes or Evernote before they pass you by.

Recently, I shared my notes aptly titled, Convivial Ideas and Convivial Quotes, with a close friend by email (ahhh...the beauty of technology), and he said he copied and pasted them into a Word document and it turned out to be 15 pages. I'd never done that, but I wasn't surprised to hear it was that long.

The other night at the bookstore, I took a peek at one author's New York Times best-selling book in the self-development section and learned that she was an avid note taker like myself. She had notebooks filled with information that made it into her actual book, but before going pro, she converted all of her notes to book form through the use of Lulu, a site that brings the world of on-line book publishing and book printing to you.

I thought that was a genius idea, because I've got journals from my childhood that could easily be converted into a series of teen novels. Who knows...maybe if I can find a senior who wants to get faster on the computer, I can ask them to type up my ten or so journals so I can get them to Lulu's printing press ASAP.

WORKSHEET

Have a Convivial Day

When you make a conscious effort to clear the way, each new day, for a blank canvas, you have the ability, mental capacity, and energy to truly create what wants to come out of you.

Use this space to create an inventory of all the things you think about, worry about, want to do, need to do…then narrow it down to the top 10 most important things you must do. Forget the "shoulds" in your life. You could leave the country tomorrow, or this world entirely, and so many of those "shoulds" won't matter.

Capturing The Muse

Where do you scribble your thought gems? Do you notice the times when they come to you more often? Is it at bedtime? Keep a notepad or your smart phone by the nightstand. Is it while putting makeup on like me (something possibly happening beneath the surface as you stare so intently and closely at yourself)?

Keep your laptop nearby or use the back of that piece of mail if you need to write it down. I've heard about people finding inspiration in the shower, but you'll need to get back to me on your solution to that scenario because stashing pens and paper could prove hazardous (wink wink).

Your muse brings brilliant, profound ideas to you at the most unexpected times and they are too valuable to take for granted and let go by the wayside. Create the habit of keeping a record of them and fleshing out the details to mark your beginning and ongoing quest to curate a more convivial life for yourself. Faith, diligence, belief, and consistent practice at documenting the workings of your mind will help you make your way down a more visible path to the life you want. Commit to creating it.

WORKSHEET

An intimate date.

Are there any hot spots or quiet café corners you've been eyeing around town? Go on a solo trip and use this page to write about your findings, thoughts, insights, fun times people watching, unexpected epiphanies, newfound wisdom, free flowing confidence it inspired in you, etc. Make it a habit. You can thank me later.

_____

_____

_____

_____

_____

_____

_____

_____

_____

_____

_____

_____

_____

_____

_____

Your Own Way Of Working

In the past, when I've wanted to prepare my mind for some creative activity (namely writing), I thought I needed just the right pen to get started, or a fancy, leather-bound notebook to put me "in the mood," or a fully decorated office space to reflect my personality and lure the creative in me to come out and play. I've even felt the need to add a glass of wine and a slice of manchego cheese, or buy a turquoise-colored vintage table to sit at, or simply avoid wearing black ever again. The closest I get to it now is the color indigo.

There are two potential sides to this coin.

You can go fancy and put a lot of intention into the tools or the things you surround yourself with when creating, and some might say it's a sign of procrastinating versus really creating something spectacular; or you can choose to keep it simple and use whatever is available to you. I say neither approach is right or wrong and shouldn't be judged either way. Everyone functions and approaches their work differently, so do what feels right to you and then…get to work.

Personally, I don't need a fancy pen, but the *right* pen does make a difference in how thoughts flow from me and onto the page. I've come to love writing on graphing paper or sketchbooks. The way the words look on paper and the amount of white space I'm given when writing gives me the sense of room to roam, to explore, to go off on a tangent vs. staying within the lines and just writing sentence after sentence in an orderly fashion. Just as artists love to go against the norm, even in their way of approaching their art this is apparent.

It's all an experiment.
Life. Art. Your life.
Have fun with it.
Do it your way.

" ... creatively ... a ...
examines our nature ... I ...
... lived at ... margins ...
... poets ...
armed mavericks, dissidents,
adventurers, outsiders, and
rebels who ask questions and bend
the rules and take risks. "

—Isabel Allende

It Starts With Belief

Deciding to write this book started with first be-lieving that it was possible for me to do, that I had something valuable to share. Many of us have these vast assumptions about authors like per-haps Stephen King, J.K. Rowling, Isabel Allende, Paulo Coehlo, or even Malcolm Gladwell: we think they had their act together from the start, but the truth is, they didn't. It takes time for the picture to come together. These were deliberate adven-turers of the mind, driven by their desires as hu-man beings, compelled to better understand the world they inhabit and the life they were given. And that need to understand the outer and in-ner worlds of which they were apart took shape in the form of a story they believed needed to be told. It's as simple as that.

> **It´s not about saying,**
> **'When I grow up,**
> **I want to be an artist,' but instead,**
> **'I am an artist, so how do I grow up?'**

—Ned, The Composer

In the last few years, I've been surrounded by all sorts of talented artists. These are creative folks who share the desire to heed the words of Ma-hatma Gandhi and "be the change they wish to see in the world." They take brave steps each new day to offer up their gifts in order for another per-son to feel seen, heard, understood, and more capable of their own gifts. It's a pyramid scheme without the scheme, a system of paying it for-ward and creating new worlds for the better.

I've mingled with these brilliant minds and can tell you this: if it wasn't for outrageous self-belief, the art they create, the messages they share, the products they make, the services they render, the overall impact they have in the world would not make it past the walls of the rooms where they began.

In order to do great things in this life, you must look within and believe that if the miracle of your existence was made possible, you can make possible another creation all your own.

I'm not even born yet. I'm still trying. I'm still pushing. I don't ever want to get to a place where I feel satisfied.

—Johnny Depp

The Challenge to Create

Creatives are hard on themselves. They're never fully content with their efforts. They don't feel good enough or that they're ever doing enough. I've heard the harsh language they use against themselves when discussing what they *have* accomplished. They give themselves no credit when all credit is due.

You would think it'd be best to hang your hat up and give up on this way of life, but this is where being almost obsessive about the vision you are called to see through becomes crucial. It serves to keep your skin in the game because, when deciding to take the path less paved, you will experience a sense of spiritual warfare within yourself.

So much can be learned from artists and visionaries alike because they hold the grand storybook of the myriad lessons on adversity, perseverance, optimism, and personal evolution.

What lessons on self-worth and personal identity could be siphoned from the ashes and rubble that constituted Steve Jobs firing from his own company as Apple CEO? How do you bounce back from such a fall? How do you find your heart's beat again? Study the response of this visionary, and you will get your answer.

Two Kinds Of Artists

There are two types of creators—the ones who know and have the clarity to produce masterpieces from inception, and the ones who have to experiment their way through life to get it. This secondary group has a wild and unpredictable trajectory when it comes to the timing of their work and when or if it will ever come to fruition.

The pursuit of a convivial life is a true journey. The world thinks they're getting a finished story, but details of a story are never fully divulged. Who gets the front row seat to the behind the scenes experience of the evolution of an artist? The artist him or herself.

It takes times to discover and understand yourself, to gather your team, tools, and resources to design the life you want. Feeling lost is a normal sentiment in this arena, but you're never truly lost. Have faith that the road beneath your feet is still unfolding and just keep taking it step by step.

I take after my father and have a natural sense of direction. I can find my way around a city fairly quickly, and when I get stuck on arriving I never think of it in terms of being lost. I am simply taking in new sights, registering new landmarks and roadways to take if I need to return down the road where I accidentally ended up. This is how life should be viewed as well.

If you are exploring and attempting to discover what you feel, you won't be able to put words or clear images together until you get your hands busy creating, building, molding, developing, and structuring a new history for yourself.

No experience is ever wasted. Every person comes into your life for a reason. You're either there to make your mark on them or let their presence impact your life. Staying open to every experience, to each person is the key to bringing all of the pieces of your life together.

The goal is to find as many opportunities to be present. That is when the worlds you want to create truly come together. Not all at once, but moment by moment. The sum of all of these experiences contributes to the grand canvas, the final masterpiece to be mounted in the hearts of those whose lives you touch.

Stealing The Present Moment

You'll hear time and again about the importance of being present, seizing the moment because that is the only thing we truly have—the *here and now*. Spiritual gurus talk about it, and scientists have studied it. Add me to the list of folks interested in maximizing it.

My interest in this subject led me to appreciate the theory of Nobel-Prize-winning scientist, Richard Feynman. He is known for the *Sum over Histories*, his best interpretation of quantum mechanics. For the record, science has never been my forte, but I was able to appreciate how this theory could be interpreted (at least by me) as a way to stay focused on the end-goal, the destination, but accept that there are infinite and unending pathways to get there and in the end, it all still adds up to one thing—the journey.

According to Feynman's Sum Over Histories theory, he sees time as *a direction* in space and thinks that an event's outcome is determined by summing together all the possible histories of that event (i.e. your life). When it comes to science, the experts and students speak in terms of particles, but I want to speak in terms of people, you and I.

Remember those experiments that you used to do in science class where you plotted points A and B on a graph and were instructed to track their progress, movement, and momentum? Yes, fun times, I know. I've said it plenty of times—you are a living work of art, the paint brush and the canvas. So, how about we make those science experiments truly relevant to your life and consider *you* as the point on the graph, the graph as your existence in the here and now, and you as the conscious creator plotting and tracking the very progress in this continually turning, twisting, evolving experiment called your life? If you chose to serve in all three roles, what sort of outcomes do you think you'd have versus choosing to be just a dot on a graph (i.e. a number in the bunch, another random face in the crowd)? Making the choice to be a highly functioning trio on behalf of the one person that you are is another form of practicing the art of convivial living.

Feynman gave examples of particles moving from point A to B. They traveled every which way, in various, fluctuating paths. The paths were never linear, but instead proved to be curved, zig-zagging. He got results of paths moving backward and forward in time, with no signs of stagnation.

This is a great visual of all the potential pathways that you can take once you make the choice to begin living your life in a more proactive and creative manner. It's never ultimately the destination, the end point, the final hypothesis on your up-close and personal living experiment; it's the journey, the learning, the connections made, the wisdom and clarity gained, and the increased pathways in your mind and in your life that are connected as a result of seeing and treating your own life as an experiment.

WORKSHEET

Go AWOL on Conventional Living

It's time to go AWOL on conventional patterns of living, the ones that haven't been serving you. Here's your chance to get a visual, a strategy, a plan down on how to begin your metamorphosis.

Take this moment to list everything that you feel needs change.

_____

_____

_____

_____

_____

_____

_____

_____

_____

Now declare potential ways to change each item you just listed. NOTE: Ways that you feel are doable for you personally.

_____

_____

_____

_____

_____

WORKSHEET

_____

_____

_____

_____

_____

_____

Now, consider and plan chain reactions on what the above changes can and will lead to if you begin implementing the initial steps toward change.

_____

_____

_____

_____

_____

_____

_____

_____

_____

_____

_____

_____

_____

Don't Count On Formal Education

The education of any creative is informal. Theories won't play as big of a role when its time to sit down and make the difference in your life or the world. It is the initiative you take, the varied life lessons you experience, the mistakes you learn from, the interests and social networks you cultivate and relationships you develop; it's the knowledge gained and so generously shared from one person to another and the discipline in which you back anything you create.

I think of my own brother who has proven that a college degree and sitting in classes can be accomplished, but to see real-life results of a convivial life you have to be driven, take risks, speak your mind, and keep your hands engaged with work that you're naturally great at and passionate about.

My brother has plenty of "mi vida loca" stories to tell you from his time growing up in inner-city Chicago. He's someone who needed to recreate himself after losing some years of his life to poor decision-making. Yet, after three years of being in business for himself as a personal trainer, he is on his way to opening up his own gym.

Here's a man who not only trains people on how to be their best physically and mentally, he also has a side business as a pastry chef, making cake pops, chocolate-covered strawberries, and cupcakes. It's hard to get a hold of him during holidays because he's busy in his studio coming up with all sorts of creative designs for his pastry clients while counting reps for personal training clients who are also possibly his pastry clients.

He had dreams to go to the Art Institute, but they didn't pan out. His life now declares, "So what!" because, even though he has no college degree, no culinary institute experience, no certification in personal training, and doesn't necessarily read up on every latest trend in any of his businesses;

he is a successful entrepreneur. And he hand-painted the art work on the walls of his gym, so I'd say that makes him an artist too.

He is relentless, passionate, well-spoken, and can adapt to any environment and find his place in it. He knows how to sell himself and treats every interaction with each new person as a potential interview. He sees each person as stock and is driven by his desire to invest in them. As a result, they make the choice to invest their time with him, and that fuels his livelihood.

How is he so successful? He gets in fear's face and blows it a kiss, taunting it, showing it that he won't be fazed. He has no desire to be a people-pleaser, though he is helping many people change their lives. He walks his talk. How did he learn to be this way? Life taught him. He has lived so many distinct lives and the knowledge gained from each world has fueled the person that he is today.

Don't get me wrong. I'm not discouraging anyone from a formal education, but I'm telling you there are too many examples of change agents in the world who have proven not to depend solely on what institutional curriculums wanted to teach them. Their lives are examples of why you need to create your own curriculum. Learn what you want to learn in the way that best suits your personality. Don't stop treating yourself to the experience of being a student once you walk that university stage. Be a student of your own life. Follow curiosity down the unique avenues and alleyways that it wishes to lead you.

WORKSHEET

Be Seen

How willing are you to be seen by others as crazy, unrealistic, out of this world, unrelenting, defiant, heretical, unrelatable, and at times incomprehensible? These are all symptoms and sentiments that artists, visionaries, and entrepreneurs on the front line of changing the world go through.

What are some fears you can face to begin showing up more in the world? List them below, then test your will to be seen otherwise. It is only then that you can begin to share your true self with others and create a convivial life for yourself.

_____

_____

_____

_____

_____

_____

_____

_____

_____

Accept today.
You are alive.
You are healthy.
You are YOU.
Worthy in every way.

> " I want to feel my life while I'm in it. "
>
> —Meryl Streep

The
Company
That Keeps
You

When I first began to construct my convivial self, I can say much of it started with simple conversations with my cousin, Tony. Tony is a meticulous man and the first entrepreneur who influenced me to take the self-employed path. He didn't mean to influence me, but how could you not be led so wonderfully astray by someone often telling you to "follow your bliss"?

I'm so grateful for all of the knowledge he has imparted to me, for the times he set me straight and I hid the tears welling up in my eyes because of my own frustration with myself. As a convivial creator who wants to experience self-actualization, you will endure the tears and keep showing up for the lesson, as well as the seemingly difficult teacher.

I took my first trip to the colorful city of San Francisco with Tony. We shopped China town and Market street, ate the best halibut ever, but what stands out the most for me was the moment Tony asked a colleague of his to share some birthday words of wisdom for my 21st birthday.

We were in our hotel room having a drink and I smiled, reaching for the phone as Tony passed it.

"Hello?" I answered intrigued.

His friend replied,

"Hello…here are my words of wisdom for you, young lady…

"All women die, not all women live."

Whoa! Talk about an ear full. Sounded a bit morbid and some might even consider it sexist, but when I thought about it, I could see how true the *not living* part can be for so many women. How many women are conditioned to fear venturing out to explore the world as opposed to men? We get bombarded with messages telling us that we're not safe, that we need a man to accompany us, that we must keep close watch of our reputations because of potential gossip. How many capable women aren't contributing their talents and skills to the workforce because their time is consumed by caring for children, elderly parents?

How many women don't schedule solo time because they are plagued by guilt? So many missed opportunities to experience ones own life is very common among women, hence the reason I took to heart the quote shared by Tony's friend. If I could help it, I didn't want to be deprived of experiences that called to me and would thus shape the person I was destined to become.

Death is guaranteed us all, but life is solely our undertaking. There are limitless ways to color the canvas of your life convivial, but you are the one who decides on what hues to pick, on the number of strokes, and ultimately how the picture ends up.

Convivial Reflections

Have you ever paid close attention to which artists and characters appeal to you? By noticing certain character or personality traits, mannerisms, and ways of expression, we can find much in common with such artists or the characters played in films that stand out to us. It's a great way to learn to embrace those traits within ourselves, because there's reason beneath the surface about why we appreciate and admire others who demonstrate the same qualities.

For example, I adore Winona Ryder as an actress because she always plays some form of an outsider. I appreciate the folks that stand apart from the crowd, who are willing to go their own way if need be. I love her role as Jo March in Little Women. When she puts on that little hat to write, it reminds me of the importance to be playful and get into character when its time to give yourself up to your art as a result of your longing for transformation.

There's also her role as Charlotte Flax from Mermaids where she declared her own religion, even though her mother was Jewish. She's simply my kind of girl. Charlotte reminds me of myself in the 8th grade. I attended an inner-city Chicago public school, yet I'd always wanted to attend a Catholic school so I could sport the cute uniform (ahh, the simplistic wants of a 13-year-old), but that wasn't in my parent's budget. Did that stop me from creating that reality for myself in some other way? No, not at all. I carried myself as if I was being privately schooled and walked the halls of Casimir Pulaski Academy in Chicago's Bucktown neighborhood, a pensive loner, appreciated by substitute teachers for my obedience, and dressed in my own unique version of that fashion ensemble—a black velvet blazer, various colored plaid skirts, black velvet platform shoes from Esprit, and the bright white tights. I even had a planner with metallic gold trimmed pages that I carried under my arm, thus capturing the eye and admiration of my science teacher. She looked at me and said, "I have never in all my years teaching ever seen a kid your age carry something so sophisticated as that planner." Mission accomplished...so I declared.

There's also Lloyd Dobler, the lead character played by John Cusack in the film Say Anything. His sincerity, humility, honesty, and that "nervous talking thing" he was so well-known for can warm any girl's heart, even the pretty high school valedictorian as the movie demonstrates.

Last but not least, young girl, Shizuku from famed

Japanese director, Hayao Miyazaki's *Whisper of the Heart* tugs at my heartstrings. She is complimented by friends regarding a song's lyrics she rewrote, thus giving it a whole new meaning. Their approval and encouragement confirms her talent for storytelling, yet like many writers, she finds trouble believing in herself. That's only a result of her lack of commitment to making the time to truly create, to focus on her "work" because she is more consumed by the mere thought of it.

WORKSHEET

Who Sparks a Convivial Reflection For You?

What artists or characters do you relate to? What are the traits that allow you to see yourself in them? Who in particular sparks a Convivial Reflection of/for you?

_____

_____

_____

_____

_____

_____

_____

_____

_____

_____

_____

_____

_____

_____

_____

_____

_____

_____

_____

Let Your Life Teach You

I wouldn't tell you to quit your day job, to pursue your passions and leave the country, your family, your spouse, your currency, your language, or the world as you know it unless I had done it. And I have.

I wouldn't tell you to take risks, to push boundaries, to put yourself in uncomfortable positions, to nurture and grow yourself, unless I do it. Writing this book has been quite the aforementioned experience.

Foreplay Versus Actual Experience

Since following my heart down this rabbit hole to self-fulfillment (and still working my way toward the light), I have participated in a number of personal development programs via books, workshops, conferences, and even one-on-one coaching with business mentors.

I sought out certain resources and tools to grow in knowledge and learn how to convert the convivial ideas that haunt me throughout my days into real-world experiences. I trusted that showing up for these experiences would lead to discovering something that didn't come naturally to me. But here's the thing…such steps toward enlightenment aren't the final solution; they are simply foreplay. Once I graduated in a sense from those savvy, well-packaged, colorfully designed and marketed programs, then it was time to

Live the experience.

The tools you use for your own personal development serve to prime you for the real work ahead. In order to make lasting connections in your mind, you have to suit up and play the game of the life you want to lead.

When you confuse theory and concepts for actual application of the knowledge, you find yourself stuck and unable to perform. What fills the space between idea and experience? It is solid work that you commit to—backed by passion, determination, perseverance, faith, a ton of patience, and unwavering optimism.

As a big-picture thinker, I can easily get caught up in the minute details of a project and not be able to move forward, but there comes a point when it's time to stop the head spinning and you just sit down and do that one thing that will propel you forward.

What's that *one thing* **waiting on you?**

Being self-aware can help you recognize when you've fallen prey to the kinds of thought storms that slow your progress or hinder it altogether.

Life is not a science or a sport: it's an art—the art of convivial living—and it must be practiced and experienced. You have to immerse yourself in the unknown to gain that understanding of what is already known deep within you.

Ask for Directions from the Driver's Seat

The moment you begin to believe that someone else has the answer you need, that is the moment you sacrifice your power.

The problem is when you place that much value on someone else's judgment, you can be steered the wrong way. You can become dependent on someone telling you what you should do. You can cripple yourself into taking action by continually relying on sources outside of yourself to make key decisions that only you know are best for you. There needs to be a healthy balance between opening yourself up to ask for help and trusting in yourself to know what is best for you.

The connections between the life *you have* and the one you want cannot be made unless you have the understanding of what you truly want and the hunger and willingness to

GO
GET
THE
EXPERIENCE
FOR
YOURSELF.

How do you begin that process? You put yourself in positions to gain the knowledge and exposure you want and need. Self-help books, workshops, mentoring, seminars, conferences, and retreats are all great ways to incorporate new patterns of thinking into your life, but any concrete changes to your life are up to you and depend only on you. All of these opportunities to improve and learn more about yourself fall under the category of self-help for a reason…because *you* are the help your self needs and ultimately relies on.

Self-help options come in all forms, but be aware of the emotions that drive you to seek various ways to improve because if any of it is based on some form of insecurity, or sense of inadequacy, or uncertainty, then you're operating from a fear. It seems ironic, because the intention is to seek assistance or the opinion of another when you feel unclear or vulnerable, yet it is in this potential mindset that you can also be swayed, influenced, or convinced to believe in or do something that isn't true for you.

I have my favorite authors and materials in the self-help industry, but I also want to point out the fact that people in my familial and social circles have just as much wisdom to impart.

If you're open to it, you can begin to see that every person you interact with has something valuable to offer you.

I don't discount the possibility of being schooled and enlightened by my friend who is an Iraq war veteran and WWE fanatic, or my Dad who cracks me up when we people-watch and pick out folks from crowded malls who resemble characters like Sharon Stone, the nerds from Lamda Lamda Lamda or the KFC colonel. It's happened once, and our shoulders couldn't stop shaking from all of the laughter we attempted to repress. I may have a blast with this man I call my father, but I know he can share the simplest of words with me and create a lasting impact. I also wouldn't hesitate to ask my rosary-wielding 78-year-old grandfather to coach me on how to have fierce confidence (though I know he'll look at me like I've lost my mind and tell me to go to church instead).

Each person has a well of wisdom to share and it's from this very act of seeing the work of art within each of them that you can extract jewels.

WORKSHEET

A Glimpse Within

We often seek information and opportunities for others to bring us inspiration, but rarely do we stop to take a look at ourselves, at the little idiosyncrasies that make up our personality, that bring joy and fulfillment to others. It is in the feedback that you get from those with whom you unwittingly and truly show up to counsel or love. It is in those activities, those conversations, those very instances that your genius reveals itself, waiting for you to return again and again to refill the well.

Take this moment to consider what others have mentioned that inspires *them* about you and be reminded that your experience matters, that you have much to offer the world.

_____

_____

_____

_____

_____

_____

_____

_____

_____

_____

_____

_____

> *Each friend represents a world in us, a world possibly not born until they arrive, and it is only by this meeting that a new world is born.*
>
> —Anais Nin

Seeing The Work Of Art In Another

There's always some place to be, an event to attend, a social activity to commit to, and many times you may dread the potential exchange with strangers, the superficial networking and small talk that can plague such atmospheres. Perhaps you fuss over what to wear or how you'll look or sound in front of people you don't know. But what if you showed up, walked into a room filled with strangers and had one intention, one thought in mind…the thought of, *How can I be of service?*

What if you saw each introduction as your opportunity to seek out, to recognize the work of art within each person with whom you had the privilege and pleasure to interact? How different could your experience be?

It is in those moments that you have the ability to extend a hand, share a story, and find the beauty in relating with another human being. Imagine the sort of world we'd live in if you took that stance with each new potential connection? This is the way of a convivial creator, someone who is all about joyful connecting and conscious action, someone who works the room with the intention to engage and delight.

Self-Help In Disguise

In the movie Bridesmaids, Annie played by Kristen Wiig, completely loses her cool at her best friend's bridal shower. Her whole life is falling apart—she loses her job, gets evicted, can't hold her own in a relationship, and now loses her best friend—so she goes into hiding. Eventually, she's paid a visit by fellow bridesmaid, Megan who gives Annie a much needed pep talk. The one line that stands apart from Megan's speech is when she says, "You're your problem, Annie… and you're also your solution."

Having someone in your life to tell it to you straight when your insecurities are running amuck is the best thing you could hope for. These are the people to appreciate in your network because, if it weren't for their bravery to speak up and tell you what you need to hear versus what you'd prefer to hear, then it'd be just another fair weather friendship. Where's the real benefit in those sorts of connections?

Cultivate your relationships and give people the freedom to share who they are with you, in good times and potentially bad. Relationships are the glue to everything in your life, and when they can get to a point when words can't come close to doing them justice, in describing the depth and sincerity they're built on, then you know you've got a rare gift on your hands.

Other Routes For Your Mind

When you feel lost, insecure, depressed, or unable to see or think straight, the best form of medicine is exposure to and experience with everything that calls your attention. The company of the people who know you best is another great antidote. Of course when you're in this frame of mind, you may not want to be around anyone, so perhaps you can consider joining a meetup group or volunteering for an organization to give back your energy in a more positive way.

When children get upset because they cannot figure something out, they throw amazing tantrums, and parents tend to do two things: tell them to stop expressing their emotions or temporarily remove them from the situation and distract them in ways that can help take their mind off the issue that's causing their emotions to run wild.

Why wouldn't you take the same approach and decide to remove yourself from a troubling moment and go for a walk, call up a loved one to see how they're doing, pick up a hobby that causes you to get lost in the moment, simply take the focus off of you?

It's easy to become fixated on an idea, a lifestyle, a job that you lost or have to take on and believe that it identifies you somehow, but as a free-thinking human being you have the power to learn to let go and decide to do differently at any time. Of course, there has to be planning involved in drastic changes you wish to make in your life, but it can be a matter of really changing your mind and moving onto something completely new.

Just Say Yes

In the movie Green Zone, Matt Damon plays a U.S. Army Sergeant in Iraq who is about to lead his troop of soldiers into an abandoned building to uncover possible weapons of mass destruction. One soldier asks him, "Sergeant, how do we know it's not an ambush?" Sergeant replies, "We don't. Get your fucking game face on."

The point is to take risks, but don't be careless. The world has no say in what you do with your life—you do.

WORKSHEET

Assess Your Risk Tolerance

"It's so fine and yet so terrible to stand in front of a blank canvas.

—Paul Cezanne (or is it?)

According to American film director, Francis Ford Coppola, risk is a way to go through life as much as possible without saying no.

Wowuh. What a way to look at risk from another perspective, huh? What are some things that you consider risky? List them here.

_____

_____

_____

_____

_____

_____

Why do you see them as risky? What emotions does this idea of risk bring out in you for the items on your list?

_____

_____

_____

_____

_____

WORKSHEET

_____

_____

How can you begin to say yes to more things that you previously saw or still consider risky? Think of the worst thing that can possibly happen. Then reassess and think, "Is *that* really the absolute worst outcome?"

_____

_____

_____

_____

_____

_____

The goal is to shake up your comfort zones a bit and get you thinking about stepping out of them more often. Share your thoughts below.

_____

_____

_____

_____

_____

_____

_____

The Power of Rain Puddles

I made plans to walk a nature preserve and was eagerly trying to get my boys into their car seats. It appeared to have rained a bit because there were rain puddles near the car, and my oldest son began making the most of his converse sneakers by stepping into each puddle. I said, "Come on, let's go now…time to get in your seat," but before doing so, my son jumped into one last puddle, then looked at me with satisfaction and joy in his eyes.

Of course, I was concerned about his socks and shoes getting soaked, but it warmed my heart to see the innocence in his desire to get his feet wet one last time.

I smiled and asked him,

"Why do you jump into *all those water puddles?*"
He replied,

"Because I like to."

A simple message from my four-year-old on how to live your life—

Do it because you like to.

When I was nine, I wrote in my first diary by declaring, "Today I ate eggs…" and I haven't stopped since. Writing is the one activity that no one has to make me do, remind me to do, convince me of the positive effect it has on my physical, mental, and emotional well-being.

I do it because I like to.

What's your "thing" to do for pure enjoyment, curiosity, self-expression?

Do what you love…
Do what makes you happy…
Do what you want…
Be who you want to be…
Do be do be doooo…

All of those phrases mean so much to each human being because everyone wants the freedom to do what they love. Granted, life and all its wonderful responsibilities require some work out of us, but for the most part, the goal of every defiant creative is to carve out a niche for themselves and create for a living, doing what they are good at, and thus the end result is creating and living a convivial life. How many people do you know who do what they love every day? How can you join them?

Live your legacy

Consider all that makes you a masterpiece. Are you living accordingly? What is so important to you that you feel you can't leave this earth without doing it?

For example, my decision to endure the tedious process of creating and publishing a book that introduces this idea of convivial living to the world was important to me because it simultaneously challenged and scared me. I had a strong desire to share a message that came into being through my own quest to awaken the work of art within me eight years ago and the story continues to unfold.

Art gives us the opportunity to seek an immortal existence; it allows us to travel to far-reaching areas of our mind, soul and spirit, to places we've yet to see, know, taste, and dream. Tap, tap, tap. We pick away at the surface of our being with each piece of artwork we produce, each business we start, each life we shape, each baby we birth…and babies are no longer just the flesh and blood kind. If we create something worthwhile, something so moving, something that can touch every soul, then the effort was well worth it and the life was well lived.

A Calling or Curiosity?

"Follow your 💚 *Art."*

Walking a convivial path requires you to be committed to the journey. You've got to know the importance of being resourceful and pro-active.

When I first began writing this lifestyle guide, I headed to a bookstore in downtown Austin with my childhood friend, Jason. He had just moved to town and was getting to know the city with me. The plan was to spend my time writing while he worked on creating a set or skit for his comedy class.

We headed to the 2nd floor and plopped our butts down in the ripped up chairs near the Creativity and Relationship book sections. I picked up a book by Dan Zadra called *Where Will You Be Five Years from Today?* I was turning the pages, appreciating the design and layout of the book along with the inspirational quotes it had in it. Eventually, I came across this page:

"An elderly man, in the final days of his life, is lying in bed alone. He awakens to see a large group of people clustered around his bed. Their faces are loving, but sad. Confused, the old man smiles weakly and whispers, 'You must be my childhood friends come to say good-bye. I am so grateful.' Moving closer, the tallest figure gently grasps the old man's hand and replies, "Yes, we are your best and oldest friends, but long ago you abandoned us. For we are the unfulfilled promises of your youth. We are the unrealized hopes, dreams and plans that you once felt deeply in your heart, but never pursued. We are the unique talents that you never refined, the special gifts that you never discovered. Old friend, we have not come to comfort you, but to die with you.

—From I Believe In You

Upon reading the story's conclusion, I got chills all over my body. I had to rub down my arms to calm the chills. That message spoke to my greatest fear, the fear of not fulfilling my purpose, my potential while here on earth.

How sad it would be to know that your life is ending and you didn't step out onto that field of dreams calling you.

Nine years prior to that moment, Jason was living in Dallas and decided to move back to our hometown of Chicago to pursue comedy. He was interested in attending Second City where many of the Saturday Night Live greats such as Tina Fey, Dan Akroyd, Gilda Radner, Maya Rudolph and many others studied. Life got in the way, and he let its strong, distracting current take him away from dreaming his little dream.

Occasionally, I'd speak with him and ask, "So, how's the comedy dream coming along?" I wanted to see him get into the arena and fulfill that commitment to himself. For a brief time, he mingled in the Improv scene and participated in a comedy troupe, but sure enough, he let life grab a hold of him yet again. He's now reached the city of Austin to start anew and as his loving friend, I told him, "There is no way I'm letting you leave this town without fulfilling that dream."

But what does fulfilling a dream really mean?

Does it mean I expect to see him famous, on Comedy Central, with his own show as his favorite Chelsea Handler? Or does it mean seeing him step onto an obscure stage during an open mic night and bomb? It means both because pursuing the experience is the first move. You've got to take the first step.

> "Luck is quite predictable. If you want more luck, take more chances. Be more active. Show up more often."
>
> —Brian Tracy

Regardless of the outcome, go after the experience, show up for the moment, meet who you will, let whatever happens happen. My friend may decide comedy is not for him, that it was just a curiosity in him needing to be explored, released from his system. Or he may discover that performing and making people laugh is his path, where he belongs, and never leave it. One thing is for sure: I am here to be a witness to his happiness and see that he feels proud of how he lives his life. This is how we as creators can support one another.

It's funny how things stay with you as you grow through life because after reading that story, I couldn't help recalling the movie A Bronx Tale where Calogero recalls the words of his mafia mentor, "The saddest thing in life is wasted talent and the choices that you make will shape your life forever."

Who would've ever imagined a mafia movie that touched on the racial prejudices of the 1950s would impart such unforgettable words to live by? How ironic that the man in real life who played Calogero ended up going to jail for several years. I'll be the first to say that his life is not over just because he went to jail, though it does leave a stain which will be tough to wash away from his past. It only means he must be creative in how he chooses to recreate himself in the next phase of his life whenever that day comes.

WORKSHEET

Love Letter to Your Muse

And the day came when the risk to remain tight in a bud was more painful than the risk it took to blossom.

—Anais Nin

Begin declaring all the experiences that you wish to count as your life's experience; all that you've been meaning to get to, all that you have in you to share, exhibit, demonstrate. The time has come to stop suppressing, stop ignoring, stop putting off.

Acknowledge it, write it, begin living your convivial life.

_____

_____

_____

_____

_____

_____

_____

_____

_____

_____

_____

{IT IS NEVER TOO LATE TO BE WHAT YOU MIGHT HAVE BEEN}

We don't necessarily discover this light inside of us—it's always been there, since the day you were born. Tell me of a time you looked into the eyes of a baby, a pure soul, whose eyes were dull? Unless that baby was lacking in love and affection, in attention and acknowledgment, then there is no denying the twinkling you see in a baby's eyes; the joy that comes through such a little body...

The spirit within us is boundless and powerful... we simply learn boundaries as we learn to "get along" in the world. We learn ignorance and complacency which hinders us from knowing and exercising what our true greatness can be. What if you could start anew, all over again?

People change every day. They change hairstyles, clothes, they change up what they eat and drink, how they speak, with whom they spend their time, the channels they fix their eyes on. Every one of those changes is driven by a choice—unless you've completely gone zombie.

So, what I want to ask is, "Why not take those choices to a whole new level?" Nothing and no one is stopping you. Except maybe you, but that's all about to change soon. Right? Riiiiiight.

I Was Blind And Now I See

When I was six, my parents converted from their ritualistic lifestyle as Catholics to a more strict Christian religion.

I remember the one and last Christmas experience I had at my grandparent's home. All of my extended family was there and I was yelling for my mother to see my new Rainbow Brite doll that my aunt had given me, and the Barbie bike I had just unwrapped with my mom's signature on the gift tag. I also remember the day my mother and father sat my brother and me down for a life-altering chat. They were there to inform us at 7 and 8 years old that we would no longer be celebrating Christmas or any of the other man-made/pagan holidays again because they were on a new,

You Are A
Living Work
Of Art

more obedient path in life, one that would take them to a place of safety when judgment day finally arrived.

I spent my whole adolescence with no Santa, no Cupid, no St. Patrick, no Dick Clark, but for some reason Uncle Sam and the Pilgrims made the cut. Just when I'd embraced my limited time on Sabbath to express what I now know was the work of art in me, we were told as a family along with the rest of the congregation that someone up at "church headquarters" had been doing their own reading, their own inner searching, extensive research, and had discovered a glitch in the Old Testament system we'd been convinced to model our lives around. The new word on this religious block was we had free will and could do as we pleased so long as God was at the heart of it all.

"WTF!?" I thought as my parents tried to explain the change to me. I couldn't believe the luck. All of the Christmas holidays I'd missed out on, the Valentine's Day school dances I cried my eyes out over because it was against my religion to participate—it all flashed before my eyes and I felt completely gypped by my church and the thought leaders my parents had listened to all of those years.

Get In Where Your Heart Fits In

It's experiences like the one previously mentioned that taught me the importance of finding your own understanding of life, divinity, culture, etc., and not shutting yourself off to the world. After all, there is no other world for you to inhabit besides this one, so why not make the most of your experience here? Why deprive yourself of fully exploring it?

This was the point when I saw how misled people can be because they are not taking the stance of a proactive creator of their own world. Instead, they are taught to put the power into another person or entity's hands. The mishaps occur in such folk's lives because they forget that they must also play a part in the evolution and progression of their lives.

You have been given the abilities that you were born with so you can take responsibility for how your life pans out. No matter what the scale or level, why be led when you can lead yourself?

> Live in tangent with nature and adjust as nature requires.
>
> —Lorie Karnath, President of The Explorers Club

Nature's Call… And Yours

At a young age, I sensed that I was special, that I was needed. I know you hear the same calling. How close are you listening?

Convivial living is in your blood. It's up to you to ignite, to nurture, and tap into it. You are a co-creator of this same world and it is time for you to acknowledge, declare, exercise, develop, and master the talents that are yours.

Is it an easel, paint, and brush that await your steady hand? Do you see your fingers taking a pen to paper, giving you the chance to convert your thoughts and existence into a tangible, shareable, inevitable realm of immortality? Is there an eager crowd waiting for you to step forward and grab the mic? To tell your story? To create the space for others to share theirs? Or do you simply need to take the stage of your own life and finally step out into the unknown, on your own, for the first time because you deserve so much more than what you've been settling for?

You have the power to create it, and the world wants what you were born to share.

The Proof Is All
Around You

There is absolute power and proof everywhere around you that demonstrates how asking for what you want and boldly going after it pays off. That's not to say that you'll get a yes every time, but the act of declaring what you want to the world will pull you in the direction of where you are trying to go. Where your attention goes is where you energies will flow.

When you allow yourself to dream, to ponder real transformation of yourself and your current reality, your eyes begin to open up to the possibilities that await you on the other side. With every risk you take or bold move you make, you will find the results validate your existence. When you are willing to say yes to the things you want, listen to your inner knowing, to what you yearn for, then life will be generous and reward you accordingly and thus prove to be a memorable and convivial experience.

WORKSHEET

FINALE: Pick a Timeline and Do That One Thing

What are your *rest of the year, next year, five year* goals?
(pick a fitting timeline)

Declare them.
Remember them. (I'm sure they're lingering in there somewhere)
Write them.
Then…

Pick ONE and begin it.

NOW. (Fact: I'm known for my bossiness.)

A Convivial Society Awaits You

As the host of this convivial world, I stand at the doorway, gesturing for you to come on through—to acknowledge and appease your deep desires, to put in the work that your dreams require, to do it all for you. Do it for those who came before you and for the ones who will follow you.

This is your time, your chance, and your choice to step into a new realm of living. Take the first step. Begin the journey. Put your talents on display. Walk on through to the other side. The Convivial Woman awaits you with open arms.

Epilogue

It will take some time for me to wrap my mind around the reality that I just wrote my first book. Not too much time though. Just as soon as I relax, then it will be time to create the next volume in this series of Convivial Lifestyle Guides.

I've only just begun. Future installments will delve deeper into more specific areas that make up our lives...such as Love - for yourself and others, Money - how to manage it and make it work for you (how else are you going to create exit plans to design the life you crave?), and much more.

I am eager to have you along for the ride as we venture down this road to convivial living.

Acknowledgements

This book would not have been possible without the Ph.D-trained and qualified mind of my (Russian bombshell English professor) friend, Nina Serebrianik. I am grateful for your natural gifts as a teacher, critic, and opinionated scholar. Thank you for being beautiful and compassionate to this self-taught writer, and for your unconditional love. You were there at the start of my journey, walking alongside me on that busy street near your apartment as I contemplated jumping the corporate cliff, and you are here today as I make real my writer's story. Our friendship is proving to have such a grand "purpose."

Then there's Julia Roberts. Thank you for saying "the word" that one fateful day. I can't forget that bossy, demanding muse with whom I committed to having a nightly writing rendezvous between the hours of 8pm-midnight (sometimes until 2am) and on weekends when I could steal the time. I especially loved those moments when she would get frustrated with me when I'd get stuck on what I wanted to say and it felt as if she just took my hand and started scribbling nonstop on the page for me. Those were the moments that flowed.

I'd also like to express my gratitude for the wonders of Mother's Day out programs, drop-in daycare, and bedroom doors that lock to keep out those adorable two year olds who only interrupt mom.

Thank you to every single person who has ever encouraged the work of art in me and...last but not least, to you, dear reader, for going on this ride with me.

Behind the
Scenes

Ambience Essentials:

Writer's Den
Best friend's hand-me-down couch
Back pillows
Candles from Anthropologie: Whipped Cream + Pear scent
Cup o' Yerba Mate / Chai Latte or a bottle of Alo

Tools:

MacBook Pro
Bic Mark Its, Ultra Fine Permanent Markers
iPhone Notes, Camera, Button to silence ringer
Instagram and iPhoto
The wonderful world-wise web

Music to fill my heart:

John Mayer, Walt Grace's Test Submarine Ride + No Such Thing
Bebe, Ella + Me Ensenara
Miles Davis, It Never Entered My Mind
Jonsi, Go Do
Beethoven, Chopin (no words means concentration for this mama)

Things I probably could have done without:

Easy access to Facebook
That blueberry muffin from Starbucks
The distraction of the first and uneventful presidential debate of 2012

About the Author

Cheryl Chavarria

Cheryl Chavarria was born in Odessa, Texas, and named after Cheryl Lynn—a '70s disco diva who reminded fans 'round the world that they "Got To Be Real." Even though her mother wishes different, she's thankful for growing up in Bucktown, an inner-city 'hood in Chicago. She's voyaged from corporate finance to off-grid travel, from magazine publishing to social media, from j-o-b-s to full-blown entrepreneurship to convivial author. She's learned to leverage her introspective nature as a source of power, rather than a social limitation. And she's learned that ignoring your muse will just make her bellow at you even louder. So you might as well listen up, and take action. You'll never regret it. She lives in Austin, Texas with her husband and two young sons.

Share

LIKE CHERYL ON FACEBOOK:
www.facebook.com/theconvivialwoman

FOLLOW CHERYL ON TWITTER:
@CherylChavarria

Shalom

www.ingramcontent.com/pod-product-compliance
Lightning Source LLC
Chambersburg PA
CBHW040126270326
41926CB00005B/85